Adaptive
Implementation

Adaptive Implementation

Navigating the School Improvement Landscape

Ryoko Yamaguchi
Laureen Avery
Jason Cervone
Lisa DiMartino
and
Adam Hall

ROWMAN & LITTLEFIELD
Lanham • Boulder • New York • London

Published by Rowman & Littlefield
A wholly owned subsidiary of The Rowman & Littlefield Publishing Group, Inc.
4501 Forbes Boulevard, Suite 200, Lanham, Maryland 20706
www.rowman.com

Unit A, Whitacre Mews, 26–34 Stannary Street, London SE11 4AB

British Library Cataloguing in Publication Information Available

Library of Congress Cataloging-in-Publication Data

Names: Yamaguchi, Ryoko, 1971- author.
Title: Adaptive implementation : navigating the school improvement landscape / Ryoko
    Yamaguchi.
Description: Lanham, Maryland : Rowman & Littlefield, 2017. | Includes bibliographical
    references.
Identifiers: LCCN 2017013318 (print) | LCCN 2017030019 (ebook) | ISBN
    9781475833508 (Electronic) | ISBN 9781475833485 (cloth : alk. paper) | ISBN
    9781475833492 (pbk. : alk. paper)
Subjects: LCSH: School improvement programs. | School management and organization.
    | Academic achievement. | Educational change.
Classification: LCC LB2822.8 (ebook) | LCC LB2822.8 .Y36 2017 (print) | DDC
    371.2/07—dc23
LC record available at https://lccn.loc.gov/2017013318

Printed in the United States of America

Contents

Preface

After decades as an educator (and even longer as a student!), I still find myself pondering basic questions about adopting or implementing "best practices" in education. Educators and social science researchers have made strides toward assembling a canon of evidence-based strategies and programs that should consistently produce good outcomes. So why is the work of educating students still such challenging work for so many?

In my experience as a teacher, technical assistance provider, researcher, and evaluator, I find that the best, most skilled educators *adapt* programs every day to meet the changing needs of their students. This notion that educational programs can be reduced to a series of scripted steps runs contrary to common sense and professional knowledge. One size does *not* fit all, and one textbook, teaching strategy, or program will never meet the needs of all teachers and learners.

This notion that adaptation is an important part of teaching and learning took root early in my career. I was a special-education teacher working with children exhibiting behavior disorders and learning disabilities. I taught in public school self-contained classrooms and residential private settings (e.g., psychiatric or juvenile detention settings) and generally had about ten students in my classroom each year. Each of my students had an individualized education plan (IEP).

Although I followed the district-sponsored curriculum, textbooks, and materials, my use of these materials with each student varied widely. In evaluation terms, my fidelity of implementation (FOI) was abysmally low. Though I started with the required scope and sequence, I created ten individualized lesson plans every week, adapting materials to fit the needs of each student. At the same time, I continuously adapted each lesson on the fly, with the ultimate lesson being shaped by the interaction between myself, the student, and the content.

Let's take the example of assigning homework. Generally, my math homework assignment came from the district-sponsored curriculum workbook. Each worksheet typically had twenty questions, ten questions on each side of the paper, and was intended to provide student practice time at home. But I knew my students had not mastered the focused attention needed to complete twenty problems, so I had to *adapt* the assignment to meet the practice goal in a fashion that was accessible and worthwhile for each.

So, what did my adapted assignments look like? For one student, I randomly selected five questions out of the twenty in the original worksheet, given the student's attention difficulties. I would rather have that student complete and understand five questions than get overwhelmed by twenty questions and refuse to do any work. For a student who had difficulty processing multistep directions, I selected two problems out of the original twenty and created sequenced miniproblems so that the student could practice microsteps to solve each problem. Without this adaptation, the student would just make answers up and hand it in, defeating my intention that she practice breaking down a problem into smaller microsteps.

In both of these examples, my FOI—use of the twenty-question math worksheet from the textbook—was low. Yet I was able to effectively adapt the material to meet the needs of the students in my classroom. My core goal was for students to gain deeper levels of math understanding, to practice independently at home, and to retain their motivation to learn. Using the worksheet exactly as prescribed would not have helped my students, and it would not have helped me meet my goal as a teacher.

When I switched over to research, the pressure to distance myself from "thinking like a teacher" was intense. I found myself needing to stop focusing on adaptation for each student and instead focus on program or strategy generalizability for all students. I could think like a teacher, or I could think like a researcher, but I could never do both at the same time.

But that is starting to change, and I like to think the change is driven by practical experiences of researchers and practitioners who are equally frustrated with their implementation experiences. Replicating or "scaling up" programs is the lifeblood of researchers, but local implementation success or "scaling down" is of paramount importance to practitioners. Marisa Cannata and Tuan Nguyen of Vanderbilt University (2015) described this research–practice divide as "tension" in design that leads to less than ideal outcomes for all parties involved. Researchers cannot describe a program that can be reliably and consistently replicated for successful scale-up, and practitioners cannot fit programs to the needs of all learners. Researchers measure and study FOI, driven by the belief that *if* the plan is implemented exactly as described, *then* known results will follow. Practitioners (quietly or explicitly) change programs all the time, driven by their belief that the plan must be *adapted* to meet the needs of their students, their communities, and their circumstances or they will fail.

Writing this book, and the many challenging conversations that led up to it, allowed me the chance to wear my teacher and researcher hats at the same time! Of course, researchers and practitioners are not natural allies in educational settings, and collaborating for success can be challenging. But *adaptive implementation* (AI) focuses on how practitioners and researchers together continue to improve their craft by systematically collecting data on adaptations, testing them out, and figuring out what works. We provide a framework for building an AI process in education, with tools and templates for practitioners to use. In the end, we hope that this book sparks a dialogue among educators as they continue to create AI processes that work for their context.

—Ryoko Yamaguchi, 2017

Introduction

Everyone involved in education wants to do the best work they can to improve results for the students entrusted to their care. We all want to improve at our craft, and practitioners have relied on research and research findings to guide what happens in the classrooms across our nation.

In the early 2000s, the passage of the No Child Left Behind (NCLB) Act signaled a shift in how we thought about and used education research. NCLB required schools to rely on scientifically based research (SBR) to select programs and adopt teaching methods. The act defined this as "research that involves the application of rigorous, systematic, and objective procedures to obtain reliable and valid knowledge relevant to education activities and programs." SBR results in "replicable and applicable findings" from research that used appropriate methods to generate persuasive, empirical conclusions.

Interpretation of the SBR clause quickly led to the development of a system to rank research in education. At the top was the gold standard, defined by randomized control trials that mimic the most rigorous research trials conducted in medicine. The federal Institute for Education Sciences (IES) created the *What Works Clearinghouse (WWC)* to serve as a repository for scientific evidence on education programs, products, practices, and policies. WWC reviewers and staff categorize the research study methodology and summarize the findings. The implicit purpose of the WWC is to review the results of "evidence-based" programs that will, if implemented correctly (i.e., with fidelity), work at new sites. In essence, programs can be replicated and scaled up.

But after more than a decade, there are few studies in the WWC that have met the effectiveness benchmark (Coalition for Evidence-Based Policy, 2013). Even more telling, schools and districts have not experienced widespread success in trying to replicate or implement these programs (Dusenbury,

Brannigan, Falco, & Hansen, 2003; Vernez, Karam, Mariano, & DeMartini, 2006). As researchers and practitioners working throughout this period, we *knew* we were limiting our options and discounting our own professional knowledge of what works in our classrooms, schools, and systems.

This work on Adaptive Implementation (AI) grew directly out of the tension we experienced trying to develop, implement, and replicate evidence-based programs in real settings. We found ourselves frustrated by the existing linear, technical protocols governing the adoption and implementation of programs. For researchers and evaluators, emphasis was placed on conducting rigorous random assignment studies and calculating fidelity of implementation (FOI). For administrators and teachers, emphasis was placed on selecting a research-based program and implementing it with fidelity. If schools changed or adapted the program in any way to make it work within their context, they were no longer using the same program and would lose the "research-based" designation. In doing so, both the researcher community and the educator community ultimately lost the opportunity to learn, improve, and innovate.

The Social Innovation Research Center published an evaluation on the effectiveness of the early progress seen from the United States Department of Education's (ED's) Investing in Innovation (i3) grants (Lester, 2017). Looking at progress from this program is key since the program represents a $1.3 billion investment in the development of replicable, evidence-based education. The report's author, Patrick Lester, found that while the i3 program achieved strong results overall, support for truly new and innovative programs was one of its weakest features. Many grantees believed that the program was not well structured to support innovation. In addition, some grantees said these grants should provide more flexibility for early-stage projects, including greater use of rapid-cycle testing, continuous improvement, pilot phases, and formative evaluations (Lester, 2017). In short, the report concluded, the technical, linear approach is diminishing innovation and stifling the evolution of new, successful strategies in the field.

Educational leaders realize that implementing an intervention or a reform is like "building the plane while flying it." AI can help them do that more successfully. AI is a collaborative model in which information flows between researchers and practitioners. AI features a set of templated tools (see the appendix) that practitioners can use to drive AI within their context. The result is a better understanding of what works in education for teachers and students in each unique context and a record of its design process.

Ultimately, this book will be useful to educational leaders and program developers seeking a new, rigorous framework for developing and improving programs, capturing professional knowledge, and using it to enhance and improve teaching and learning.

SCHOOLS: A COMBINATION OF TECHNICAL AND ADAPTIVE SYSTEMS

John Otterness, a NASA rocket scientist turned math teacher, said, "Teaching is not rocket science, it's much harder!" (Otterness, 2009). Why is teaching much harder? Because rocket science involves parts that fit and systems that function exactly as expected, but education is far more complex, dynamic, and, therefore, interesting. Otterness (2009) went on to explain, "Rocket science was easy. We built only what we knew. We designed for what we expected. It was state of the art, but it was not beyond that. When something didn't work the way it was supposed to, we knew that we needed to look for the part that didn't perform. We knew what we were designing and what outcome we wanted. Everything was controlled to achieve those results."

This type of **technical systems** thinking, where parts are engineered to fit, maintains an outsized influence on the educational practice field. To improve student outcomes, a school can purchase a new intervention (the part). Using technical systems thinking, we assume that proper implementation or fit will consistently, and repeatedly, yield the same results (Berman, 1978). But in real-world schools and classrooms, we know that this is not true. Every day brings new surprises and challenges for educators.

The layered complexity of educational systems makes technical approaches impractical. Every state official, superintendent, building administrator, and classroom teacher takes directives and mandates and molds them to fit their professional view. Implementation of the common core standards provides a classic example of how a single message (or set of standards) is shaped, rearranged, and reprioritized to fit local context. Much like the children's game of telephone, even a very simple technical mandate is substantially changed as the message passes down the line.

Ultimately, all efforts in education should impact the teacher–student–content interplay. But what that interaction looks like is the result of a complex system that seamlessly weaves together policies, programs, and influences from the national, state, and local levels (Cohen, Raudenbush, & Ball, 2003). When that interaction is faulty, finding the part to fix is never as clear or as straightforward as in a technical system. You can't isolate the broken mechanism and engineer a new part to fit. Interventions like the School Improvement Grant (SIG) program failed in large part because they tried to use this technical fix approach (Dragoset et al., 2017).

Alternatively, **adaptive systems** are driven by feedback from experience as they learn and grow (Berman, 1978). In adaptive systems, designers begin with an understanding of what the end product, or outcome, looks like. They know where they want to end up. Often, early iterations of a program design are "best guesses," with the designers knowing they will learn during implementation and come back and make the design better. Think about that little computer we all carry around with us all the time. You probably upgraded your phone when your older model was damaged or began working less effectively for some reason. The newer model you hold in your hand undoubtedly does some things your older model did not, and it probably does others faster and more efficiently. Yet, you know and accept the reality that this latest model phone is not perfect, and your future phones will be even better. This type of "design thinking" drives the technology sector (IDEO, 2012; Madhavan, 2015; Penuel, Allen, Farrell, & Coburn, 2015). Every application and device is always under development, with new versions designed in response to feedback from users. Technology is always adapting to user needs.

Researchers at Brown University noted the need to embrace adaptive change in an early look at how NCLB changed the educational environment as state education agencies shifted from a monitoring to a capacity-building role (Dwyer et al., 2005). They discerned "The shifting definition of organizational roles ... have catapulted states into territory in which past practices and procedures and existing knowledge are inadequate. An outcome is that states have been forced to make initial responses, learn from them, and make incremental adaptations that move them towards desired goals. They are functioning in conditions ... requiring adaptive rather than technical approaches to leadership" (Dwyer et al., 2005).

Adaptive systems in education rely on professional knowledge and experience to continuously improve the model. Deviations from "implementation as intended" are not viewed as missteps or failures, instead they provide valuable information regarding ways to improve the model and better fit a given context (Bryk, 2016; Kilbourne et al., 2014). Adaptation relies on the professionalism of educators, where teaching—much like leading—is dynamic and always being adjusted to the rhythm of the classrooms and the needs of individual students (Heifetz, Grashow, & Linsky, 2009).

WHAT ARE YOUR CORE GOALS?

Teaching and learning are complex, as rocket scientist turned math teacher John Otterness explained. We can control some elements, but we cannot control them all. Every leadership change at the national, state, or local level prompts new educational priorities that trickle down to teachers and students. A high priority today (e.g., third-grade reading levels or fifth-grade math scores) is replaced with a new urgency to focus on something else tomorrow (e.g., high-school graduation rates or early education).

Educational priorities shape core goals for districts and schools. Core goals are the big, important drivers of a system; they are typically nonnegotiable and must be implemented. Think for a moment—what mandate has your school, district, or state enacted in the last three to five years that impacted teaching? Examples abound. It could be as specific as improving the passing rate in Algebra I to something as vague as focusing on "the whole child." Practitioners and researchers typically don't have control over the core goals, but they do have to figure out how to make that goal attainable.

AI is a design engineering approach that helps build a process to reach your goal and improve that process through multiple iterations. AI creates a systematic framework for teachers, leaders, and researchers to collaborate as they tinker, adapt, and improve. AI helps us take a core goal and design engineer a process to reach it.

ARE YOU SCALING UP? OR SCALING DOWN?

The movement to require adoption of research or evidence-based practices rests on a powerful but implied assumption: that success on a small scale can be copied and should lead to wider use (scaling up). We have the strong desire to believe that what happens in "the lab" can be replicated at scale in "the field" (Burns, Appleton, & Stehouwer, 2005; Hulleman & Cordray, 2010). The funding that drives research in education promotes this assumption and funds smaller developmental programs with the understanding that they will be ready for replication within a few years or funding cycles.

Practitioners, on the other hand, are rarely interested in scaling up or replication. Their concern is with implementation on-site in their classroom, school, or district. We characterize this approach as "scaling down"—in the sense that educators want to learn how to make programs work and fit in their local context, with their students.

The concern of scaling up from researchers and scaling down from educators represents the tension between the researcher–practitioner partnerships (Cannata & Nguyen, 2015; Cohen-Vogel et al., 2015; Penuel, Allen, Farrell, & Coburn, 2015). However, both concepts are important. Taken together, they make a powerful argument for collaboration between researchers and practitioners as a way of ensuring that both elements are addressed. Information about replicating programs at new sites is vastly enhanced by learning about the context-specific elements used in the past and understanding how other practitioners adapted and changed the program. AI serves as a common process and a common language for practitioners and researchers to use together—with an emphasis on a collaborative team approach (the AI team).

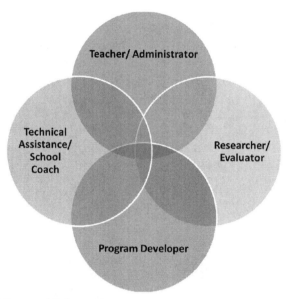

Figure I.1   AI Team and Roles

ADAPTIVE IMPLEMENTATION TEAM

AI grew out of frustrations experienced by the individuals who created this book. We had the opportunity to delve deeply into the education system through our multiple roles as teachers, administrators, researchers, evaluators, technical assistance providers, and school coaches. From teaching special education students, English Learners (ELs), and general education students to serving as local and state education administrators, we bring a unique perspective wearing multiple hats in education. The trick was to figure out how to wear all these hats at the same time.

This vantage point of multiple experiences and perspectives in education allows us to understand the value of both research and practice, and how they interact synergistically. As the pressure and focus on "research-based" interventions and approaches grow, we found information flowing in one direction only—from research to practice. Research organizations are increasingly promoting collaboration through programs like researcher–practitioner partnerships used by the National Science Foundation and the "research alliances" supported by the U.S. Department of Education (ED). The driver of these partnerships is always the researcher or evaluator, promoting a "research and evaluate" point of view to scaling up what works (Cohen-Vogel et al., 2015; Penuel, Allen, Farrell, & Coburn, 2015).

Many "collaborative" partnerships are still characterized by researchers delivering research to practitioners in a dutiful fashion. This is often followed by practitioners working to add this new information to the extant pile of research-based practices they've been told to integrate into their teaching. One could be forgiven for mistaking these less-than-effective partnerships for delivery services that may or may not feature a site visit. Researcher–practitioner partnerships all too often mirror this sort of limited interaction. Truly collaborative partnerships can identify problems and develop programs to address them. Thus, prior efforts to bring researchers and practitioners together have often missed an opportunity to use data to improve the adaptive process, which naturally occurs and is essential to effective teaching and learning.

AI is a highly collaborative process and requires a team in the school setting (figure I.1). The team consists of professionals doing the work (e.g., teachers, school leaders, teacher leaders, etc.) and professionals providing support (e.g., researchers, data experts, etc.). It is in the day-to-day experience of cycling through the AI process, with data at the ready to inform the next steps, that we can start to identify and learn from what happens in an adaptive system like education. Learning from adaptive systems cannot happen when researchers "push-in" to the school for their research, nor can it happen as a solitary activity among teachers.

The AI team is an essential element to the AI process. The team may include practitioners, coaches, researchers, evaluators, program developers, and so forth. For people in these support roles, the AI team is a new way of thinking about their work. For practitioners, teaching is no longer a solitary activity but a team sport demanding new, rigorous ways of thinking. It is the practitioners who are driving the action, and through the AI cycle, it is their professional knowledge and experience that is utilized (Goodwin, 2015). For data experts, research is used to support the AI process with essential information gleaned from various data sources, regularly referenced and revisited to meet the needs of the AI process (Cohen-Vogel et al., 2015). For school coaches and technical assistance providers, coaching is primed by research and data, with continual formative data and feedback from data experts to the practitioners (Park, Takahashi, & White, 2014). For program developers, implementation is not for fidelity's sake but for continuous improvement (Bryk, Gomez, Grunow, & LeMahieu, 2015; Park et al., 2014).

ADAPTIVE IMPLEMENTATION CYCLE

AI is not a wholly new concept. It has primarily been used heretofore in behavioral and healthcare settings (Kilbourne et al., 2014), discussions of public policy (Berman, 1978), and applications to leadership (Heifetz, Grashow, & Linsky, 2009). These applications have focused more on studying adaptations made to programs and services after the fact. As we apply it to education, AI focuses on education practice improvements in an existing setting (e.g., a typical school). We initially borrowed some aspects from Fidelity of Implementation (FOI) study methods, but AI offers a different tool, with a different purpose, for a different job. AI is designed to help developers, researchers, and practitioners—with a given set of intended outcomes and an intervention in development—hone in on optimal design (i.e., endogenous factors) while also defining the optimal intervention setting (i.e., exogenous factors).

Time in the classroom taught us that the surest way to fail our students was to doggedly use the same instructional methods with them all. Our experiences as researchers have taught us that the same is true of systemic change; one size does not, cannot, and should not fit all (Bryk, Gomez, & Grunow, 2010; Bryk et al., 2015). So, AI focuses attention on using data, information, and professional knowledge to solve specific problems of practice—similar to the way successful educators approach teaching to meet the needs of all students.

AI applies design engineering principles to the work of improving education. Design engineering is a decision-making process, often iterative, that applies knowledge and experience to achieve a stated objective. This approach does not supplant the current plan-do-study-act model of continuous improvement in education (Bryk, Gomez, & Grunow, 2010; Bryk et al., 2015; Park & Takahashi, 2013) but builds on it by laying out tools and protocols teams can use to achieve their core goal. AI embraces the fact that, as an organic system, education requires fluidity and flexibility in its approach and practice to be successful.

In applying this design engineering approach to educational improvement through the process we call AI, we created a five-step iterative process centered around the core goal (figure I.2). AI does not end with the completion of one cycle but instead continues to adapt or evolve organically with the program or strategy being addressed. Throughout the AI process, the consistent theme is on improving and documenting what works.

Step 1: What Do We Need to See?

The first step in developing a process to help you reach your core goal is to identify waypoints—those things you can see that guide you closer to reaching your core goal. Core goals tend to be big, nonnegotiable, overarching, and difficult to achieve. Your team will need to find a way to identify the things they can do to help move closer to the core goal or end point. If your goal is to improve high-school graduation rates, your AI team might focus on a

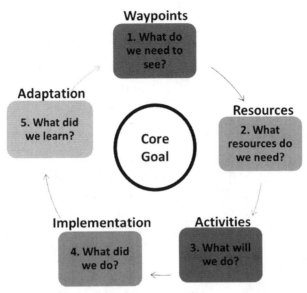

Figure I.2   Adaptive Implementation Process and Key Questions

smaller set of students with special needs. This might lead your team to set a waypoint of reducing the dropout rate by 10 percent for students in your specific program. So far, so good, right? We're all used to setting measurable objectives.

Let's consider an example from daily life. As you come home—exhausted from a full day at work—the dreaded question arises, in a pressing tone: "What's for dinner? I'm starving!" This question strikes fear in many and has directly resulted in the development of a multibillion-dollar fast-food and prepared-foods industry. Your core goal is to see a quick, healthy dinner on your table! Everything you do is aligned with this core goal (figure I.3).

The main question is this: *What do we need to see* … on the dinner table. If a teenager shares your abode, the answer is, "I don't know, just make something good, like take-out pizza." If you have a toddler, the answer is, "Chicken nuggets shaped like dinosaurs." Regardless of the age, you have identified the waypoint you need to reach: to see nutritious and delicious food on your table! This thought process of deciding what to have for dinner is done on a daily basis, and it typically takes only a few minutes.

In education, we have a similar thought process that starts as simply as, *What do we need to see our students (or teachers) do?* This simple question can be very hard to define and may take much longer than a few minutes.

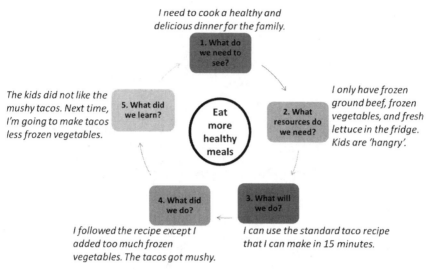

Figure I.3   Adaptive Implementation of Making Dinner

Let's assume your district is reinvigorated to use new state standards to prepare students for the rigors of college and career. If that is the core goal, what do teachers need to see students do in the classroom? These waypoints should be informed by data and research—during a collaborative discussion between researchers and practitioners.

In our expanded discussion of step 1 (What do we need to see?), we will detail how we can move from traditional, "strategic plan" core goals of a school system—which are often inspirational, though less than functional, mission statements—toward a specific set of waypoints based in research and data, that can be consistently observed (and measured).

Step 2: What Resources Do We Have?

Our second step focuses on taking stock of the current situation by identifying and cataloguing resources and constraints. Using dinner as an example, this is the same as asking yourself, *What is in my fridge?* And, *How much time do I have to make dinner?* We have a decision point here. If you don't have anything in the fridge, your option is takeout for dinner or a trek to the grocery store or market. If you have enough compatible ingredients, you may have a home-cooked meal waiting to be assembled. Constraints always depend on the context—the teenager or toddler will soon reach the "hangry" threshold and, therefore, you may only have fifteen minutes until they lose it.

In education, discerning what you have involves taking stock of the resources, supports, and constraints that you or your team contend with: teachers, staff, infrastructure, tools, space, volunteers, curriculum, textbooks, assessments, and so forth. Any planning must take into account these resources and constraints, or it will risk being divorced from the contextual realities that we all face. In this chapter, we will describe the process to identify and catalogue resources and constraints through a modified needs assessment. In addition to identifying what we have or lack, our AI approach will help identify what we have that could be adapted or turned into a resource. Creativity in utilizing the resources at hand is a hallmark of successful schools, and we capitalize on this through needs assessment.

Step 3: What Will We Do?

This step features the set of action steps needed to get to the waypoint (from step 1), given the resources and constraints (from step 2). It is important to note that in AI, this is the third step. Usually, we want to go straight to this step. "Let's just do it! Time's a-wasting!" But, if you think about it, we often move through steps 1 and 2 in an instant. Let's take the dinner example: we think through the waypoint and resources in a split second. Then, in this step, we quickly figure out the recipe that fits this specific situation. I am going to select my tried-and-true recipe to make tacos, with clear steps to cook the ground beef, shred the lettuce, and serve with tortillas (three key components).

In education, this is usually the activity impacting student, teacher, or school leader behavior that you *think* will lead to the waypoint from step 1, given the resources and constraints from step 2. School staff and program developers live in this realm of answering the *What will we do?* question. These are the action steps proposed to reach the waypoint, where we create interventions to "get inside the black box" of improving student achievement.

In this chapter, we will present the Design and Action Plan (DAP). The DAP is a road map that displays the key components (activities), given the resources, constraints, and waypoints. By creating the DAP, we will also identify data points for each key component so that we can keep track of what we planned to do and what we actually did.

Step 4: What Did We Do?

Have you noticed that we often only ask, "What did I do?" when we get in trouble or when something did not go according to plan? In AI, we always ask ourselves what we did because it is part of our learning and improving process. Knowing what worked as well as what didn't work are equally valuable parts of this learning process. This step is highly data-driven, with each component aligned with data and information gathered by the AI team. It's not enough just to adapt; we must also understand why we're adapting and how our adaptation will impact practice and help us reach our waypoint.

Continuing with our dinner example, the question here is whether you followed the recipe to the letter or adapted it by adding or substituting ingredients. If the resulting dinner was well received, noting the substitution in the recipe will help you replicate the successful dinner at a later date.

In education, it is doubly important that we document changes and adaptations and codify all aspects of what was done to assess how these worked. But innovations that are not understood and documented are often dismissed as a one-off, a flash in the pan, or merely a fad—if they are even noted. In this chapter, we will outline the process of documenting what was done. Herein lies an important distinction of our AI process. AI works to understand the strengths, weaknesses, and future opportunities for improving an intervention. It is not evaluative.

Step 5: What Did We Learn?

But wait! There's one last step in our cycle, and this step is a critical component in the improvement process. Following the dinner example, we don't make dinner once and never again. We repeat the process, learning and improving as we become more experienced. At the same time, we don't typically make the same dinner every night. We are always adapting to meet the changing needs, wants, and tastes of our household members.

In education, we have the same situation. Students change, as do the instructional strategies that work best for each individual. Standards and curriculum change as well. As such, we try an intervention out, we adjust, and we learn. It is this adjusting, documenting, learning, and improving that is at the core of our AI process and at the heart of this book. In this last step, we review the data to figure out what to improve and adapt. The temptation is to ignore this step and move straight into another cycle without review or reflection. While this would be a cycle, it is not an *improvement* cycle. We continue to lose valuable information about what works if we do not look critically at what worked, when, and how and then adapt for our next cycle. This chapter will focus on identifying the lessons learned and adapting a model while maintaining focus on our core goal. We will document the process of using the data on implementation gathered in step 4 to build lessons learned and steps to improvement.

Adaptation cycles should take as long as they need to surface meaningful feedback. In some cases, that might be just a few days. For example, a team might decide to use a quick verbal assessment as an exit strategy to measure student understanding of the day's content objective. Within a week, a team may have garnered enough experience for them to decide if the strategy is worth holding on to or if they should abandon it and explore other formats. In other circumstances, adaptation cycles might be much longer.

The authors of this book have been working together on a grant-funded program designed to improve academic outcomes for ELs, Project ExcEL (Excellence for English Learners), and many of the ideas expressed here were developed through the day-to-day work of implementing the project and reaching toward success. We've drawn out examples from Project ExcEL to illustrate each step in the AI process and so include an abbreviated case discussion of Project ExcEL to help you put the examples in a real, ongoing context.

Following the case discussion, we delve into the details of each step in the AI process. With each step, we highlight the role of the AI team and include tools and protocols to make your work simpler and more efficient. The appendix includes AI tools in template form for educators to use in their own AI process.

CASE STUDY: PROJECT ExcEL

Many of the ideas expressed in this book were conceptualized during long and sometimes frustrating conversations about the implementation of a comprehensive school reform model we developed to improve outcomes for ELs. Project ExcEL was originally established in 2007 and is currently in its third formal iteration. The authors of this book have worked together for years to develop the Project ExcEL model, improving the effectiveness of the model while struggling to understand what supports that effectiveness in different contexts.

AI arose organically as a concept from the tensions arising among researchers, program developers, and practitioners. Researchers were focused on implementing a defined model with fidelity, while practitioners were determined to shape the reform model to meet their context. We all brought different goals, experiences, and viewpoints to the school reform table, and we all answered to different entities. Ultimately, we knew we needed a different way of thinking about the implementation process, one that honored the expertise of researchers, program developers, and practitioners together.

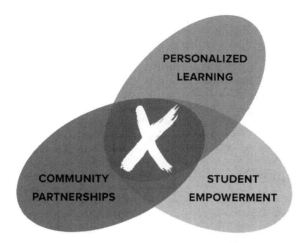

PERSONALIZED LEARNING

COMMUNITY PARTNERSHIPS

STUDENT EMPOWERMENT

Figure I.4

As we went through iterations of ExcEL, we began to notice that certain approaches were far more effective than others. At the outset, we developed a Comprehensive School Reform model that focused on the traditional forms of school improvement (i.e., providing new resources and professional development and working with teachers to improve instruction and pedagogy). The interactions were unidirectional, where the program developers provided training and support to teachers. The goal in these interactions was that teachers would then, in turn, use the new knowledge and skills in their classroom, which would ultimately improve student outcomes. This approach reflects the most common model in educational reform, though we were noticing that the results were not as effective as we had hoped.

In its current iteration, Project ExcEL is actively and intentionally shifting to a multidirectional focus, including and honoring the expertise of the teachers, program developers, community partners, and researchers. The program brings together personalized instruction, student voice and ownership, and community-based learning under the direction of a collaborative leadership team facilitated by the program developers at the University of California, Los Angeles (UCLA) (figure I.4).

A simple but fundamental shift underlies the developing success of this approach. ExcEL is an attitude more than a program. ExcEL is not a prescribed set of practices or strategies but an approach that allows educators the time and structures to use their own expertise to address the individual challenges facing their students. A deep understanding of the strengths, needs, and aspirations of each student is explored, and flexible programming is designed to meet their needs. Our overall goal is to use AI to define the inflexible elements of the project (i.e., the scaffold that will support scaling up) and the flexible, context-specific elements (i.e., the scaffold that will support scaling down and success in new sites).

AI is the way to determine what we can and cannot do and understand why. We now understand that the ExcEL model will *never* be perfectly described, but the ExcEL process will keep us on the journey to success. With that in mind, we offer the ExcEL story as a way of illustrating the concepts and steps of AI. The project overview is provided here, and you will find references and examples used throughout this book.

The Excel Model

Project ExcEL is an enhanced, comprehensive design that addresses the unique and urgent needs of schools and districts with populations of ELs—districts that are struggling to provide a comprehensive, rigorous education for the newest members of their communities. The project employs a data-driven, tiered approach to instruction that builds on community partnerships to create personalized, expanded learning opportunities for students. The core philosophy is one of enriched activities and wraparound supports focused on success for each student.

Teams of teachers work together to discuss and tier EL students. They proactively address urgent and immediate needs as well as improve pedagogical and other supports for all students. Established community partners provide academic, social, and emotional supports to students and their families as needed. Teachers, program developers, and community partners work to identify barriers to engagement and success. The program developers facilitate ExcEL team meetings that include district leaders, teacher teams, and community partners focused on discussing a single primary question: What can we do to help *this* student succeed?

ExcEL has its origins in a committed group of educators who believed we needed to transform our approach to working with ELs. Even in schools and classrooms where "best instructional practices" were being practiced, positive impacts were small and marginal. We believed there was a better way—and that transformative change would only happen when *every* teacher became a teacher of ELs and had the knowledge and skills to make that a reality.

We first put these ideas into practice with the support of a National Professional Development (NPD) program grant from ED in 2007. The Excellence for Connecticut's English Language Learners (EXCELL) model focused on building the instructional capacity of teachers in four Connecticut districts (New London, Montville, Norwich, and Stratford). EXCELL provided comprehensive, job-embedded coaching and professional development to mainstream teachers in grades K–12. Support was delivered in the context of school-based professional learning teams. EXCELL led to demonstrable improvements in student outcomes. In several cases, EL students outperformed their native English speaking counterparts on the Connecticut Mastery tests (the annual state assessments).

The success of this pilot led to a commitment to model improvement based on the initial experience. Developers sought, and received, another development grant under the i3 program. Project ExcEL, funded by ED in 2013, works with secondary schools in Ossining and Tarrytown in the state of New York. In addition to the core principles of working with mainstream teachers and facilitating the delivery of coaching and embedded professional development, Project ExcEL added three elements:

- a systematic way of tiering students based on progress (similar to a Response to Intervention [RtI] approach);
- ensuring that every EL student is part of a small learning community; and
- partnering with community agencies and establishments to provide a wider array of supports for students and their families.

Critically, this improved model is now the subject of a rigorous research study that is establishing and quantifying the effectiveness of the model on student outcomes. Interim results on implementation showed a high FOI and captured valuable input from the field that has been used to reshape the project moving forward. Exploratory impact findings from the third project year are indicating an increase in the average state test scores for ELs.

Additional funding under ED's National Professional Development (NPD) program was received in 2016, supporting the development of a K–12 site in Shelton, Connecticut. The ExcEL Leadership Academy builds on the New York project, adding a structured pathway for teachers to receive an English as a Second Language teaching endorsement. The ExcEL Leadership Academy is also intended to develop into a professional learning center where others can come and learn about the model.

ExcEL is the only comprehensive model designed to improve outcomes for ELs in a public, integrated school system. Each iteration of the ExcEL model has created valuable opportunities for learning and shaped our own thinking about replication and sustainability. We have identified specific areas for continuous improvement and iteration as we hone in on the comprehensive aspects of the model.

We are in the midst of implementing ExcEL. As we work our way through iterations of the ExcEL projects, we continue to learn what works and what doesn't work at *each specific site* as well as how to allocate and reallocate resources in order to best meet the needs of students. Staff changes, funding sources dry up, better materials are created to replace what we have—any of these variables can easily derail a program if we have not provided the flexibility to overcome them. We knew that we needed a systematic way to quickly analyze what specific activities were working and what was not— while building the process to evolve and adapt to changing conditions.

Step 1

What Do We Need to See?

The Chinese philosopher Lao Tzu wrote, "The journey of a thousand miles begins with a single step." Committing to a journey and taking that first step can be a daunting challenge. But once you've started you immediately need to figure out where to go next. How do you orient yourself and not get lost on your journey? You need to define waypoints to mark your progress.

A waypoint is a reference point, and if you were navigating on land, it would refer to a physical location or entity, something tangible you can see and move toward. Can you imagine yourself hiking deep in the woods without a marked path to follow? You know where you started and where you want to end up. Maybe your goal is to summit the mountain in front of you. Easy, right? You just need to keep moving upward!

But if you have ever summited a mountain, you know the path is rarely direct. You may encounter thick woods, swamps, loose rock fields, and other formations that you are going to need to go through or around. Your hike is not going to follow a straight line; it's going to meander a bit. What can you do to prevent getting hopelessly lost along the way? You will set waypoints, identifying physical markers you will be able to see and progress toward.

If you were climbing a mountain, you would use a topographic map and note large, observable features along your route. So, when you start out, you are not aiming for the top of the mountain to the northeast of your starting point; instead, you are focused on reaching a large boulder field due north from your starting location. You can see it easily, and, even in the dense woods with limited visibility, your compass will help you stay on track to the north. Hiking to the boulder field first ensures that you avoid the large swampy area and delivers you to an area where you can safely cross the river and continue on your journey.

Humans have been using waypoint markers for a long time, with villages and gathering spots often adopting the name of the marker or unique geographic feature (like Foggy Bottom, in Washington, D.C.). But waypoints are not limited to physical structures. Project management has a counterpart to the waypoint; project managers create timelines and set milestones leading to the final result. Setting waypoints or creating milestones allows us to confidently make incremental progress without fear of getting lost shutting the process down. When you start your journey by saying *I need to get to the large boulder field*, you are describing a place you think you can reach. Importantly, it's clearly described, and you'll know it when you see it.

Waypoints, or *I need to see* statements, also allow you to learn from missteps and mistakes. Climbing a mountain or stopping students from dropping out of school are both daunting tasks. But when the tasks are broken into smaller steps, you have the opportunity to reset missed waypoints and chart a better path.

We all set goals, whether it is a personal goal to eat more healthy or a school accountability goal (e.g., to decrease achievement gaps). The journey toward achieving that goal starts with step 1—what do we need to see? *We need to see* statements remain fixed for the adaptation cycle, but each cycle concludes with a reexamination of the question as team members look to create a record of what they have learned during implementation and decide if they want to adjust their initial question or move on to the next waypoint.

HOW AMBITIOUS SHOULD WE BE?

It would be an understatement to say there is a great deal of information and advice available on how to set goals and targets. A quick Google search on "setting good goals" yields several hundred million results! When we discuss AI, we distinguish between core goals (imposed from the outside) and project level or AI goals. It is worth remembering that core goals are the big, important drivers of a system; they are typically nonnegotiable and must be implemented. For our purposes, we are not seeking to set core goals; we'll leave this task to national, state, and district leaders. But we do need to consider the scope of our *we need to see* statements and where they fall in a range or continuum of goals.

For Adaptive Implementation (AI) waypoint-setting, we suggest that you are your team be bold but not *too* bold. At one end of the goal-setting universe we have the big, hairy, audacious goal (BHAG). BHAG is an idea conceptualized in the book *Built to Last: Successful Habits of Visionary Companies* by James Collins and Jerry Porras. According to Collins and Porras (1994), a BHAG is a long-term goal that changes the very nature of a business' existence. These are the types of singular visions that can drive organizations toward fundamental change. In an educational setting, you might postulate the elimination of achievement gaps or a 100 percent high-school graduation rate as a BHAG.

At the other end of the goal-setting universe, we have SMART goals (Doran, 1981), goals that are specific, measurable, achievable or attainable, realistic, and time-bound. SMART goals encompass targets you know you will be able to hit and are best used to create action steps that will ensure that you get where you want to go. SMART goals have recently gained favor as part of teacher evaluation and accountability processes. SMART goals are achieved through careful planning and hard work but do not necessarily require risk or new learning.

An effective *we need to see* statement falls somewhere between these two extremes. It is not too safe, and it will require new learning and the application of some elbow grease. It is not so risky or removed from current reality that it makes implementation attempts likely to fail. Overall, it must suggest a possible course of action.

IDENTIFY WAYPOINTS

By asking ourselves, "What do we need to see?" we start identifying waypoints that are measurable and observable and aligned with the core goal. For example, if our core goal is to prepare students for college and career readiness, there are a lot of things needed to address this important goal. As such, it can quickly become overwhelming.

When you create waypoints to help you climb a mountain, you identify where you want to end up. Then you pull out topographic maps to help you navigate a feasible route to the top. You consult with other hikers who have attempted the same summit and listen to their advice. You check the weather forecast. You plan multiple waypoints, mapping out alternative routes to the top so you can adapt to conditions on the ground, but you never deviate from your goal of reaching the top of the mountain.

In the same way, the AI team must map out a series of waypoints to help them reach their core goal. Too often in education we identify our first waypoint without understanding how it fits in with the overall journey. If luck is on our side, we might end up with small pockets of success. But these successes won't be coordinated and most likely won't move us closer to our core goal. Using research and professional knowledge as a map is an important part of identifying a waypoint aligned to a core goal.

If your core goal is to prepare students for college and career, research in education will show you that completion of Algebra I by the ninth grade is a key early indicator of high school graduation (Allensworth & Easton, 2007; Balfanz, Herzog, & Mac Iver, 2007; Neild, 2009). Aha! That's tangible, measurable, and could be a great place for a high school team to start. *You will be able to see* an increase in the passing rate for that course, and you will be further along in your journey toward your core goal. Of course, your Algebra I efforts will have a much greater impact if they are integrated with efforts aligned across grade levels and schools. Your map, drawn from research and professional knowledge, tells you the introduction of proportional thinking in the elementary school is another important waypoint.

Waypoints in AI are small steps that scaffold and build on one another (Bransford, Brown, & Cocking, 1999), advancing you toward your core goal. If the core goal is college and career readiness, we can develop waypoints for students at each grade level, such as

- fifth grade: understanding proportional thinking,
- sixth grade: mastering proportional thinking and reasoning,
- seventh grade: applying algebraic thinking,
- eighth grade: passing Algebra I, and
- ninth grade: passing Algebra I or Algebra II.

Even experienced mountaineers think and plan multiple waypoints for their journey to the summit, being ready to react and adapt to whatever conditions they encounter. AI teams also need to map out contingent routes for reaching their core goals even though they address them one at a time.

CREATE YOUR ROAD MAP

Your first charge as an AI team is to create *we need to see* statements to guide your work (textbox 1.1). But you need to ensure that *your* waypoint aligns with the road map and supports achievement of the core goal. No matter where you find yourself on the educational landscape, it's highly likely that someone else created your core goal for you. It is like the little fish getting eaten by a large fish getting eaten by an even larger fish. Teachers get core goals from administrators, administrators get them from policymakers, and researchers get them from funders.

Textbox 1.1 Adaptive Implementation Team

The AI team works together to create the road map and identify the waypoints. Team members share their professional experience and conduct research together to develop reasonable pathways with the potential for success. The waypoints should be important to all members of the AI team.

As you begin to plan out and implement your program, you need to think through the potential steps in your journey before deciding on your initial waypoint. Just as in chess, you choose your first move by considering the array of possible subsequent moves.

The AI team works together to create the road map and identify waypoints. Team members share their professional experience and conduct research together to develop reasonable pathways with the potential for success. In mountaineering, the best waypoints are permanent, accessible, and clearly visible from long distances. Likewise, there are common characteristics that the best educational waypoints share.

FIVE CHARACTERISTICS OF STRONG WAYPOINTS

Without a clear direction and action statement of what *we need to see*, it becomes impossible to learn from, and adapt, *what we do*. Strong *we need to see* statements share five common characteristics:

- They focus on things that are important to you.
- They focus on things you can do.
- They demand effort and new learning.
- They are built on evidence of student need.
- They are built by the people doing the work.

The AI team should meet, often multiple times, to identify their waypoints. During your discussion, review the five characteristics of your waypoint using the scale in figure 1.1 to ensure you are developing the best *we need to see* statement possible.

Setting your waypoint statement (i.e., defining what it is you need to see) is an iterative process. Your statement will get better as you use the AI process to work the problem through. You will learn and your understanding will evolve. Like Goldilocks, you will eventually find just the right statement for you and your team.

It doesn't impact what I do every day, and I can't really affect it. No ownership. Wasting my time.

Meh! I'm a good sport and I'll play along.

This is why I went into education! And it affects what I do every day. It's going to make me better at my job.

Figure 1.1   AI Scale to Create the "Right" Waypoint

PROJECT ExcEL EXAMPLE

Let's look deeper into the process that the ExcEL AI team used to draw their map and select waypoints. Project ExcEL began with a clear core goal: after all, "Excellence for English Learners" is right there in the name. The core goal is to improve the college readiness of English learners (ELs). To reach this goal, the AI team discussed several waypoints, including providing personalized and differentiated education services to ELs and improving the ability of teachers to respond with new instructional strategies.

Teams of teachers at each project school worked together to discuss and tier students based on their individual challenges and strengths. The teams brainstormed ways to meet these needs, bringing in outside resources when and where needed. Eventually, the AI team agreed that they needed more professional development to teach EL students. Eureka! The waypoint was to secure more professional development for teachers. Through the AI process, the waypoint was crafted into an action statement: *We need to see more effective instruction in our classrooms.* This waypoint was developed after a series of discussions, meetings, and collaborative learning experiences with the AI team and ExcEL teachers.

Waypoints Focus on Things That are Important to You

In the first year, the teachers who participated in ExcEL (we will call them ExcEL teachers) decided they should offer training in instructional strategies to their colleagues, those teachers who were *not* part of the project. But guess what? Not surprisingly, people showed up for the training because they were good sports, but no one really took anything of substance away. For the colleagues, learning about instructional strategies for ELs was not at the top of their priorities list. If it were, these teachers would most likely have also volunteered to be an ExcEL teacher.

Waypoints Focus on Things You Can Do

ExcEL teachers began to ask themselves what they wanted to learn and improve and realized they didn't want (or need) new knowledge. What they really needed was the time and support to implement the knowledge they already had. What they needed was the chance to work with their peers. They did not want to learn from experts (i.e., via didactic learning). They wanted to sit with colleagues and learn together (i.e., via collaborative learning). This signaled a change in their thinking, focusing on their own practice and classrooms instead of how their colleagues were teaching.

Waypoints Demand New Effort and Learning

This shift in defining the purpose of the activity was powerful, and it resulted in the development of a "table-hopping" strategy. Each team member worked on a classroom activity or strategy that interested them and became an "expert." Each team member then had the chance to share their activity with peers by literally sitting at a table and chatting with whoever was interested. Experts opened their classrooms on designated days and invited peers to come in and observe the activity in real time. This approach demanded that everyone put effort into the learning; the option of being a passive bystander was removed.

Waypoints are Built on Evidence of Student Need

When ExcEL teams meet and discuss ways to meet individual student needs, specific instructional areas emerge that can be addressed through this organic approach to professional learning. This characteristic seems to state the obvious—of course it is about student need! And yet, it is very easy to take our eyes off the ball in education, and we offer *lots* of professional development activities without any real evidence that these activities fill a professional need for us or, by proxy, our students.

Waypoints are Built by the People Doing the Work

Another key characteristic of effective *we need to see* statements is that they are built by the people involved in the work or the problem. While the project road map was constructed at the beginning of the process, the development of this particular waypoint has been strongly shaped by the teachers involved in the professional learning activities. The initial statement, *We need to see more professional development*, was created by the project designers. It only evolved into a more useful statement (*We need to see more effective instruction in our classrooms*) once the people engaged in the work (the teachers in the schools) pushed the change.

Step 2

What Resources Do We Have?

Your Adaptive Implementation (AI) team has figured out your first waypoint and defined it in terms of what it will look like when you get there. You're on your way! But wait—before you can get going, you need to make sure you have the resources needed to sustain you through the journey.

Determining what resources are available and how you can use them is a challenge, and many programs fail at this point. Every school has stories about program failures. That one person sitting in the back of the room, arms folded, staring intently, already knows that the "research-based reading program of the month" is not ever going to take root at *this school* because resources are already stretched thin. She's listening, and she hears a lot of additional tasks to be performed, but she doesn't hear anything about new supports.

She already knows the following:

- The district is never going to approve purchasing the full set of classroom materials for all teachers. So dedicated folks will try their best to share workbooks, but ultimately they will be forced to abandon the effort when materials run out.
- The reading interventionist position has been unfilled since the school year began, and there are not enough adults to manage the small student groups needed to work with the new program.
- Many classrooms are overcrowded and noisy, and there just isn't enough space to assemble, much less effectively manage, small groups.
- The online component of the program designed to monitor individual student progress requires a full complement of working computers in each classroom. Teachers have been shuffling computers between rooms for months in an effort to meet even the most basic classroom technology

needs. The wear and tear is beginning to show. Cable ends are broken, and peripherals are now missing.

Sound familiar? We are looking at the results of failing to manage and align money, staff, materials, and technology resources to support program implementation. Within the AI framework, our intent is to think deeply about the resources needed for success. Because we are focused on getting to our first waypoint, we also realistically acknowledge existing constraints and find ways to substitute or work around barriers. AI teams also intentionally seek out opportunities for securing resources in creative ways.

In order to avoid failure before even starting, we need to be realistic and creative about what we have and what we can reasonably be expected to do with it. What kind of funding is available, and what can we spend it on? Do we have the necessary materials? Do we have the staff? Are we able to provide the time needed to do something? Can we ensure everyone is properly trained? Realistically, we never have all the resources we need. This is why we must also be creative. How far can we stretch what we have? What can we repurpose to meet our evolving needs?

Resource management is typically defined as the "efficient and effective" deployment of resources when and where they are needed. Resources are generally classified as financial, human, inventory, or technical—in education we might think of them as money, staff, materials, and technology. The *management* of resources implies that allocation is not static, and an AI approach benefits from constantly balancing what we have with what we need (figure 2.1).

Returning to our dinner example, when our harried working parent thinks about what to serve for dinner, she quickly reviews what's on hand in terms of ingredients. *Hmmm, there's ground beef and fresh tomatoes in the fridge, along with a bag of frozen veggies in the freezer.* The glare of the hangry teen elevates the time constraint, but she rapidly considers other limitations as well. *The microwave is still on the fritz, and my favorite baking dish is still soaking in the sink from last night. But my saucepan is clean and sitting on the stove.*

By mentally managing the resources available to provide dinner, she has narrowed her choices from the *possible* to the *likely* to be successful. Dinner will be both efficiently prepared and effectively satisfactory.

Gathering and properly allocating resources to support program implementation can be a challenge, and programs are frequently abandoned because they cannot provide necessary support. Faculty and staff simply return to "business as usual" when the new program does not provide time for training or enough books for everyone to use. Using an AI approach, we take a realistic assessment of what we have and mobilize our resources in the best way possible to meet our needs. This resource management is not simply a

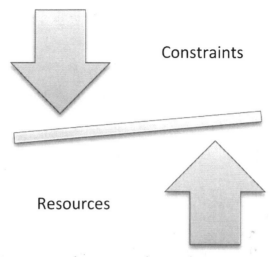

Figure 2.1   AI Management of Resources and Constraints

"one and done" deal; instead, as each AI cycle progresses, we reconsider our resources—to add new resources, examine what was most efficient, and determine if we had the resources to do what we need. We also use the power of the collaborative team to figure out how to fill any identified gaps (textbox 2.1).

ASSESS WHAT YOU HAVE

Regularly reassessing resources can help prevent us from returning to simply falling into the same patterns of doing what we have always done. It is human nature to enjoy what we do well, after all. There's nothing wrong in relying on routines that have been successful in the past, but they should not preclude the chance to evolve and grow. Therefore, it is important to think creatively about what is needed for improvement.

Categorizing resources as **general** (common resources available to many or most schools) and **specific** (locally important, context-specific, or those most germane to the implementation) helps to broaden our thinking. Resources always need to be considered when balancing *what we want to do* with *what we will be able to do*.

Schools and districts generally provide a set of similar, basic resources; these are **general resources**. Budgets are established that provide for salaries and materials. Staffing levels are determined based on student populations and administrative needs. Buildings, furniture, and books are provided.

Technology to support educational and management needs is also in place. General inputs might be thought of as background inputs; they exist without additional, specific effort from the AI team.

These are all important, basic needs, and we take general inputs for granted until they are scarce or hard to access. For example, an unfilled position on the teaching roster might have a major impact on the intended programming and serve as a real, perhaps, insurmountable constraint. Along the same lines, an antisocial, unapproachable data manager effectively limits technology as a resource. Opaque purchasing procedures, extant purchasing agreements, or fiscal staff simply stretched too thin may all limit funding options and the mutual understanding and cooperation necessary to move forward.

Locally important, context-**specific resources** are resources that may only be important at a local level to a specific project. Specific inputs, with resources targeted to support the implementation effort, might come from partnerships, grant funding, philanthropies, civic groups, faith-based organizations, nonprofits, parent–teacher groups, or other service organizations. There might be specific areas of federal, state, or local law and regulation that need to be considered.

Textbox 2.1 Adaptive Implementation Team

The Adaptive Implementation (AI) team works together to identify the resources needed for implementation. They discuss constraints that limit resource access and opportunities for new or reallocated resources to support their work. Creativity within the AI team is necessary to identify opportunities—going beyond what is always done to what could be done. A teacher or school administrator is ideal for facilitating the resource discussion.

Sometimes we overlook context-specific resources: for example, failing to think about skilled parent volunteers as a resource to extend academic remediation efforts. Perhaps the most often overlooked context-specific resource is the knowledge and ability of the people doing the work. Researchers and practitioners bring a variety of knowledge and experience to the table. This combined knowledge can be a tremendous resource, given the opportunity to tap into it. In fact, it's a lot cheaper than bringing in outside experts, and you end up with shareable knowledge tailored to your setting. Plus, it makes your team members feel better about their role! Similarly, we all recognize the benefits of student peer learning; let's not forget that this is equally valid with adults.

ASSESS WHAT YOU DON'T HAVE

Whenever you are thinking about resources, honest conversations about implicit and explicit constraints are necessary. We need to have assumptions challenged so that we can dig deeper into the realities underlying them. Constraints almost always include the obvious things like lack of funds and time; it is rare to find any school that has "extra" time and money lying around! But the more powerful constraints may be the implicit, cultural forces that operate in the background just beyond awareness. Every classroom, school, district, or organization has cultural norms that can dramatically influence how resources are allocated. Even though everyone might be aware of these, they are rarely addressed. Naming something makes it real and clarifies your thinking about it.

A framework is useful to help expand thinking about constraints, both implicit and explicit. Explicit constraints are tangible, known elements. They are generally specific and clearly understood by all parties:

- Contractual constraints often arise from teacher or labor agreements. Most educators operate in an environment where their time and assigned tasks are clearly described (and limited). Adding new tasks cannot be done without an adjustment to time requirements or compensation. Additional contractual constraints include things like agreements governing building use, facilities staff, and mandates associated with purchasing supplies and services.
- Policy constraints frequently arise from tension between "how we've always done things" and new initiatives requiring flexibility or change. When New York State mandated a co-teaching model for English learners, the requirement to provide the same services for students with special needs sometimes results in the English as a New Language (ENL) teacher "pushing in" to a small, self-contained class, where there are already several adults working together. Compliance with the various policies may not be coordinated, and sometimes the result is a confusing array of "help" provided to students with severe needs.
- Logistical and structural constraints are obvious limitations, yet curiously they are often ignored. Many cotaught classes were created by *adding* ENL students to an existing English Language Arts (ELA) or math classroom in spite of the fact that there may not be enough chairs or desks for the additional students. Beyond furniture and classroom size, supplies are often in short supply. The schedule routinely shows up as a structural constraint. School schedules are notoriously inflexible and are almost always built around the needs of the adults in the building.

- Financial and human resources are finite, limited resources, particularly in education. Again, new programs or initiatives almost always demand a shift in how existing resources are deployed.

Implicit constraints are more tenuous, and different people may perceive them in very different ways. A common example of an implicit constraint often arises when programs are implemented specifically dealing with "sub groups" or small numbers of students with special needs (such as English learners [ELs]). School boards may be wary of publicly acknowledging these programs or even accepting outside resources that might be perceived as diverting attention (and funding) from the mainstream population. Another common implicit constraint is the reluctance of some school districts to add grant-funded staff positions. Each implicit constraint needs to be viewed within the local context and weighed accordingly. For a challenge to be addressed or even effectively mitigated, it must first be recognized and understood.

It is helpful to carefully distinguish between policies and practices. When we continue to do something because that is the way it has always been done, we are simply repeating past practice. Policies, on the other hand, are largely silent about *how* things get done. For example, the requirement to hold a teaching license is a *policy* across most of the nation. But how you earn that license is all practice, and you can earn a license from a professional school, through an alternative pathway, from life experience, or even from a few undergraduate courses in emergency situations. Obviously, we cannot break the law or violate policy in order to try something new, but we can certainly consider the inherent flexibility of our practice.

This stage of the AI model can be the most frustrating and can also easily make us feel like giving up. Nobody relishes the idea of doing more with less! Having an honest discussion about our resources and related constraints should not be an excuse to bail out; instead it should provide us with a clear, realistic idea of what we are actually capable of doing. When our mountaineer sets off to a waypoint, icy conditions might force them to slow down or seek a new path. When we set off on our way to a milestone, we need to make sure we can navigate our way with the resources at hand. If the schedule does not allow teachers to meet during the day, then we need to find a way to meet using technology or before or after school. Rather than banging our heads against the wall about what we can't do, let's focus on what we can do. This is where we start to take stock of our opportunities.

ASSESS WHAT YOU COULD HAVE

There are also implicit and explicit opportunities that should be explored when you are talking resource management. Again, a "devil's advocate" or an education outsider can often help assess or consider implicit and explicit opportunities. The rhythms of established institutions and systems can lull individuals and groups into ways of thinking and assumptions that can, and often do, undermine their effectiveness. Intentionally revisiting the list of needed resources is as important as consistently collecting and using student assessment data. This is particularly true since it is highly unlikely that all the necessary resources will be listed at the outset. Just because a resource is not in place when the program begins, it doesn't mean that it might not become available. Opportunity really does knock sometimes, but, as Louis Pasteur noted, "Chance favors only the prepared mind."

Opportunities to secure resources might come in the form of grant resources, community or volunteer partners, or other entities inside or outside the school or district. Identifying these potential sources of revenue or help isn't always easy, but it helps to think about other organizations that might share in the mission of the new program and be willing to contribute and possibly collaborate. Requesting contributions for new undertakings shouldn't always be a veiled request for money or materials. Brainstorming with a like-minded outside organization can help schools build community goodwill and support while also offering the chance to access heretofore unconsidered resources or partners.

Of course, the opportunity to reallocate resources needs to be explored as well, and this is often as challenging as looking for new resources. When we open a discussion about reallocation, we are going to step on a few toes, because it necessitates a discussion about doing things differently. But, without having this discussion, we become the place that just keeps layering new initiatives and programs without ever changing or adjusting what exists.

Opportunities can also include existing resources that could be repurposed to meet your needs. Principals often do this at the school level where they have a bit more control over their budget and staffing, but it takes a strong team to recognize potential opportunities among existing resources.

Principals can also collaborate across the district or across the school in ways that are often not considered. For example, a principal knows that the current social studies teacher is also certified as an ELA teacher. This is a resource in staffing that could be utilized to integrate literacy into social studies to improve reading outcomes. Working together, a school principal or lead teacher could easily work with a guidance counselor to recruit parents for a "college and career" day to talk about their career pathways or start a mentoring program.

Think about this for a moment—we only bring in new programs *when we want to change outcomes*. By definition, that has to lead to doing (and sourcing) things differently. There are explicit and implicit opportunities all around us. Every school exists as part of a larger community. While the level of engagement with community may vary with each school, the need for and value of it does not. Explicit opportunities encompass things like existing training time (e.g., professional development days) or targeted grant funding for materials. Implicit opportunities often touch on reallocation issues that can be difficult to talk about or politically sensitive to adjust. However, without additional funding, these implicit opportunities can offer schools a creative way to look at what they could have.

The AI framework makes resource management explicit by listing resources needed for the program, along with a consideration of *opportunities* and *constraints*. The Resource Management Tool (figure 2.2) is a simple, useful guide for the discussion. Every group considering resources needs a "devil's advocate" or an individual willing to ask the "dumb questions." The status quo doesn't change until someone asks, "Why?"

Money

Carefully consider the type of money you're seeking to access or use. Examples include:

- Are you using grant money that can only be used for certain things?
- Are you following federal, state and local audit guidelines in your proposed use of the money?
- Are there other funding sources that might cover the same things?
- Have you considered fundraising to obtain additional resources?

While money truly is just another tool to be used effectively and efficiently, it is a resource that requires conversations with fiscal/financial staff to ensure appropriate usage and effective tracking of expenditures.

What you have (Resources)	What you don't have (Constraints)	What you could have (Opportunities)

People

Carefully consider staffing needs over time.

- Unlike money, materials, or technology, staffing requires an extra measure of careful thought because it involves the well-being and security of people and their families.
- Whether you work in a union, right-to-work or other environment, you're entrusting people with important tasks that need to be matched with skills, commensurate pay and benefits, and a funding stream.
- While it may be the norm in education to slide individuals around as grant funds and special pots of money become accessible, thereby bridging staffing and funding, it is not an effective way to recruit and retain committed professionals.
- Does the intended role of a new staff member require highly specialized skills, or would this present an opportunity for community engagement and volunteer opportunities? Is there a community partner who could provide similar expertise?

What you have (Resources)	What you don't have (Constraints)	What you could have (Opportunities)

Materials

Materials are often combined or conflated with money, but the need to split these two categories of resources is tantamount to understanding the nature of resources available to you.

- Materials may be included in the fees or funds expended when purchasing or obtaining models or packages of resources—don't be afraid to ask leaders and vendors what is included (is it digital? can you copy it?), when materials will be

Figure 2.2   Adaptive Implementation Resource Management Tool

available, and what the cost of additional materials is. Get this in writing when feasible and appropriate.

- Materials may be available as donated goods or at a reduced price through local affiliates.
- Materials may have already been purchased or may be purchasable through extant purchasing agreements or existing programs. Don't duplicate efforts because you're afraid to ask.
- Is there a community partner, state/federal office, or philanthropic organization tasked with providing resources in this area?

What you have (Resources)	What you don't have (Constraints)	What you could have (Opportunities)

Technology

While technology has traditionally been fetishized in education, it may help to plan for technology needs as if it is merely another type of resource. However, given purchasing constraints and existing agreements, technology may need to be tracked separately based on your local context. Though used to frame technology here, the following questions can be used for the categories above as well:

- What critical need does the technology fill? Can this need be filled with extant resources?
- Is the technology worth it? It doesn't take many gimmicky do-dads to get to a full-time teacher's salary (especially when one adds in service contracts, extended warranties, etc.). Ensure that the technology adds real value.
- Again, is there another source that could fund this technology?
- If the technology didn't exist, how would you do what you want to do without it? Is the answer more cumbersome than the purchasing process, the expenditure of funding, the training needed to effectively use the technology, and the need to maintain the technology?

What you have (Resources)	What you don't have (Constraints)	What you could have (Opportunities)

Figure 2.2 *(cont.)*

PROJECT ExcEL EXAMPLE

Identifying and gathering resources played a major role in the implementation of Project ExcEL, particularly when New York State (NYS) developed new mandates without providing funding to support them. Midway through the implementation phase of Project ExcEL, the New York State Department of Education issued a set of regulations (referred to as Part 154) requiring major changes at the school and classroom levels. Specifically, ENL teachers were mandated to deliver ENL instruction using a "push in" approach, rather than pulling ENL students out of class for stand-alone language support. In practice this required an ENL and content area teacher to work together with a common set of students. Few questioned the logic behind the move, and ExcEL teachers generally agreed that it was better to keep ENL students in the classroom with their non-ENL peers, but many questioned whether they had the resources to meet the requirements properly.

Using an AI approach, ExcEL districts were able to reframe the issue from a technical challenge (a logistics challenge that can be "fixed" with a modified schedule) to an adaptive challenge (one that needs experimentation and adjustments to ensure students are getting what they need in the classroom). Employing the AI approach helped schools bridge the gap between accountability and improvement and allowed for district context, teacher expertise, and student needs to drive the conversations about how coteaching could improve overall outcomes for EL students.

AI teams at the ExcEL schools created their waypoint statement: *I need to see ENL students learning language and content together in the content area classroom.* Next, team members began an in-depth discussion of what they needed to get started on their journey. Highlights of their conversations included the following points:

- Coteaching is a staff-intensive process and requires additional ENL staff to simply meet the scheduling demands. Quality coteaching also relies on sufficient time for coplanning, which in turn impacts the budget as teachers are afforded additional planning hours during or after school.
- Both new and existing staff members require training and support to learn how to effectively coteach. Matching coteachers can be tricky, and careful attention to the interpersonal dimension is crucial. Supporting teachers over a year or longer and providing them with effective feedback for improvement requires expertise and patience. Identifying teachers interested in this practice and committed to new learning is foundational to the overall success of the initiative.

Table 2.1 Resources Identified as Important to Coteaching Implementation

	Resources Needed
Money	Additional staff required; financial support for coplanning time
People	Identifying the "right" people and providing training and support
Materials	Language development programs aligned with content area
Technology	Student management systems, teacher coplanning platforms

- The curriculum guides used by ENL teachers were not aligned with the concepts and skills taught in the content area classroom. This meant ENL teachers often needed to revamp their instructional programs to align language development with the content area program. In many cases, content area teachers also revamped their instructional programs to reinforce language development skills. In almost every case, a need for new instructional approaches was evident.
- Technology resources were important in a number of areas. All teachers needed access to student classification and assessment data in the content and language areas. In some cases, existing technology systems were not designed to allow coteachers access to the same student data, so even the creation of a joint roster became problematic. Teachers quickly seized on technology as a valuable communication tool for their own use in coplanning.

Once the teams established their "wish list," they began a discussion of the constraints. As the old adage reminds us, "if wishes were horses then beggars would ride." Educators as a whole are excellent wish makers, but they are not always very good at getting horses. But AI team members are creative and skilled at finding their waypoints, and they took a realistic look at the opportunities and constraints that influence resource availability *before* moving forward with a plan (table 2.1).

The ExcEL team members created an excellent, well-thought-out plan (their wish) identifying all the resources available, but they could not bring it to the implementation stage (no horses). It was only after considerable work on the opportunities and constraints influencing coteaching was completed that a better (adaptive) approach began to emerge. The teams were fortunate to have people in the role of "devil's advocate" who were perfectly willing to ask "dumb" questions and upset the status quo.

ExcEL schools did not have the required ENL teachers on staff (the resources), and *need more teachers* went on the list of resources. Requesting additional staff members was anathema, even though it was absolutely required to implement the mandate. The requests were eventually approved, but it took a full year to request funding, identify, recruit, and hire new ENL teachers. There were also implicit constraints operating. The budget request had to be carefully constructed to ensure that it conveyed a message of equity for students; administrators were cognizant of potential pushback from the representatives of other student groups. Additionally, some ENL teachers silently resisted efforts to collaborate when they felt that their content specialty was devalued or made secondary to the traditional content area. Some of them felt they had been demoted to the role of paraprofessional.

Table 2.2   Resource Management Chart for Coteaching

What You Have (Resources)	What You Could Have (Opportunities)	What You Don't Have (Constraints)
Additional staff required; financial support for coplanning time	By eliminating some stand-alone ENL classes, we can free ENL teachers for coteaching opportunities.	We're a small staff and over-extended.
Identifying the "right" people and providing training and support	We can tap into expert coaches from UCLA as part of our grant support.	Having observers offer feedback in the classroom is problematic and can impact the teacher assessment process.
Language development programs aligned with content area	We can draw on grant resources intended to support Professional Learning Community meeting time to extend common planning time and align content.	Many ENL students have not had exposure to Regents-track content area classwork, so we don't know what the pacing will look like.
Student management systems, teacher coplanning platforms	We have "experts" on our staff with a lot of skill in using Google Classroom as a collaboration tool.	It is difficult to get up-to-date, comprehensive data from the student management system.

ENL: English as a New Language, UCLA: University of California, Los Angeles

Table 2.2 captures the full "opportunities and constraints" discussion from one ExcEL school as they worked to implement coteaching. As a reminder, the mandate for coteaching was introduced during the third year of the grant implementation, so it did not appear in anyone's plan or list of resources. The staff worked closely with the program developers, researchers, and practitioners to reallocate existing grant resources. School coaches offered additional time and feedback to coteachers, and stipends for team Professional Learning Community (PLC) meetings were partially redirected to support coplanning time. The coteachers themselves came up with ways to communicate and collaborate and shared their ideas with colleagues during PLC meetings.

Where an AI mind-set does not prevail, staff hobble along and grumble at the unfair expectations of implementing new programs. Resources needed for coteaching were not provided by the state, so a compliance mindset moves ahead without them. What is nominally coteaching becomes two teachers working independently in one classroom, both are pretty unhappy, and student needs are not met. Without AI, the coteaching model is clumsy and burdensome and student outcomes remain static or fall—all because there is no mechanism in place to consistently learn from what works, and what doesn't work, during implementation. Where the AI mind-set prevailed, administrators and teachers found the resources needed to support coteaching, resulting in stronger implementation of coteaching models and improved student outcomes.

So, we have our map, we know our first waypoint, and we have the resources needed to get us there. We are finally ready to get moving.

Step 3

What Are We Going to Do?

Step 3 (*What are we going to do?*) focuses on developing a clear story about your program or intervention. The process culminates in the production of a Design and Action Plan (DAP). By this point, we have a clear understanding of where we are headed (*step 1—what do we need to see?*) and what we need to sustain our journey (*step 2—what resources do we have?*). Given these factors, this chapter focuses on how we create a map.

Planning for success, mountaineers always factor in things like pace, elevation, and weather. Start out too fast, and you'll need to quit before you reach your waypoint. Start out too slow, and you'll end up trying to navigate in the dark. Therefore, the answer to the guiding question, *what are we going to do*, should not be met with "Let's just get going!" The key components and activities need to be thought through and should make logical, theoretical, and practical sense.

We use two tools or processes to plan and coordinate our activities over time as part of this Adaptive Implementation (AI) step. The first is a pro and con assessment (PCA) used to narrow down our choices of activities from everything we can think of to the best possible choices. Once the activities are identified, we collect the activities and key components into a second tool. The DAP builds out the road map to our first waypoint, constructed in step 1, by adding details about how our journey will proceed. Key components (what we will do) and activities (how we will do things) are planned.

CONDUCT PRO AND CON ASSESSMENT

By the time we have clearly identified our waypoint and resources, it is natural to want to get started by jumping right in. After all, you've probably done something just like this many times before—but slow down! If you jump in too fast, you might not see the best path to the waypoint. When you move ahead without careful consideration at this stage, you are likely to default to something you've done in the past and miss this valuable opportunity to brainstorm new or different approaches. As educators and leaders, it is all too easy for us to want to push progress as hard and fast as possible and to do so in ways that aren't always the most efficient or effective.

The science and art of organizational development offers protocols to compare the merits of different approaches and settle on the best way forward. These include things like strengths, weaknesses, opportunities, and threats (SWOT) analysis, needs analysis, risk assessments, and others. We find that the PCA is simple, direct, and reflects the philosophy of AI—ultimately, we are always moving forward with our best guess at what will work. PCAs reflect, capture, and inform the dynamic team processes focused on improving complex, organic social systems like schools and classrooms.

The history of approaches to education reform and improvement is littered with proposed solutions that involve better trained teachers, more engaged parents, applying technologies, better textbooks—the list goes on and on. But, when the solution is not tightly aligned with the waypoint and the resources, you end up with an answer in search of a problem. Take a look at the What Works Clearinghouse (WWC) (wryly nicknamed the "What Doesn't Work Clearinghouse" by many practitioners due to the number of interventions found to have no effect) for its plethora of examples of misaligned or poorly implemented interventions, methods, and strategies (Seftor, 2016). At all levels of the system we default to doing what we know how to do well or what has worked in the past.

AI exists to break this tradition of implementation failure in education. The PCA template shown in table 3.1 requires that each proposed activity be clearly defined and stated simply. The PCA starts with the observable waypoint (from step 1), right there at the top. The potential activity is clearly specified by the people who will be responsible for carrying out the proposed work, with resources stated. A sample activity with requisite details would read as follows: "Daily after-school literacy tutoring by homeroom teachers. Provided to Tier-3 students for fifteen minutes per day, for a total of 45 minutes per week. Instructional materials provided by local Kiwanis." Note that the description of the proposed activity must be detailed enough so that the AI team thoroughly understands the resources needed to carry out the work.

It is important to note that the identifying challenges (the cons) associated with an activity do not disqualify it. If we waited to develop the perfect activity, we'd never do anything at all. Honestly discussing the challenges can be a challenge in itself, since they sometimes sound or look like judgments on practice or even individuals. To be clear, a PCA is not a listing of individual or

Table 3.1   Pro and Con Assessment Template

Observable Waypoint: Student Assessment Shows Growth in Grade-Level Reading

Activities and Key Components	Pros (Resources: Money, People, Materials, Technology)	Cons (Resources: Money, People, Materials, Technology)
Potential Activity 1: *Literacy tutoring for level-3 students* (Money Needed) *Teacher stipend* (People Needed) *Provided by homeroom teachers* (Materials Needed) *Fifteen minutes a day, after school, three times a week. Instructional materials from Kiwanis.* (Technology Needed) *None*	Intensive instructional support is likely to be effective. Results will spill over into other content areas. Homeroom teachers know the students' strengths and challenges well. After-school approach does not take away from other instructional time.	Teachers may be unable or unwilling to commit to after-school tutoring. Students who take the bus home cannot commit to staying after school every day (no late bus) and may have other responsibilities such as a job or caregiving.

organizational weaknesses. Rather, challenges are factors to keep in mind to help ensure successful implementation. Think of the con section as a checklist of items to consider thoroughly. Sometimes there are items on that list that preclude successful implementation, but sometimes they provide an opening for ways to think through or around barriers. Don't shortchange this discussion just because it may be more difficult to discuss the challenges.

The PCA process creates an excellent opportunity for some out-of-the-box thinking by the AI team. Given the chance to brainstorm and consider new or unusual approaches, teams can surface great ideas! Encourage team members to think through every idea, even if it seems impossible or silly at first glance. Don't forget to look through the eyes of multiple stakeholders, including students, families, teachers, administrators, policy makers, and business and community members. Remember, this is a critical juncture where you should slow down and look at all your options before proceeding on your journey.

The completed PCA offers you a menu of activities and components. You don't have to pick just one (the best); you are more likely to choose to meld several strategies into one action plan. When we look back over programs that have met with success in schools and classrooms (i.e., those outlined in the WWC Practice Guide series) and on our experiences as educators, solutions that work in a complementary, synchronous manner tend to have a greater impact on student outcomes. For example, in Project ExcEL, team members address teacher development, coaching supports, student wraparound services, community partners, and an overall cultural shift at the same time. Using the PCA brainstorming method, we can identify possible components of the larger solution while balancing these with our context and resources to visualize how they can work together.

CREATE A DESIGN AND ACTION PLAN

The complexity of education settings requires that we understand the underlying connections between components and activities so that we consider the connections between our solutions and the systems that can support them. This is the time to leverage complementary strategies and ensure efficacy and efficiency. Our evolving understanding of the need to emphasize evidence-based practices requires that we open the black box, break down what we will be doing, and describe how it all fits together. Gone are the days of merely going with your gut and following your instinct. While AI raises the importance of professional judgment and experience in program design and implementation, it balances those elements with what we learn from educational research. Our improvement designs are stronger when we tap into this growing array of tools to help us understand and measure student learning.

We all have experience developing these types of plans, even though we call them by different names. Action plans, lesson plans, strategic plans, conceptual frameworks, theory of change models, logic models, and probably many more. Logic models have emerged in recent years as a required, omnipresent element for educational interventions. But they are not the only, or the best, guide to designing a program that is adapting and evolving.

The Problem with Logic Models

The term "logic model" is rather loosely applied to many types of models these days. The Kellogg Foundation (1998, 2004) lays claim to the first use of program logic models. They define logic models as "[a] picture of how your organization does its work—the theory and assumptions underlying the program. A program logic model links outcomes (both short- and long-term) with program activities/processes and the theoretical assumptions/principles of the program" (W.K. Kellogg Foundation, 1998). Logic models were intentionally established as a tool to guide program evaluation and accountability. So even though they are frequently used as planning tools, they are much better suited for monitoring and reflective purposes. Figure 3.1 provides a look at the basic structure of most logic models (W.K. Kellogg Foundation, 2004) using planning for a family vacation as a focus.

The overall goal in this example was to build and maintain good family relations, and the planning team laid out a clear, and logical, argument

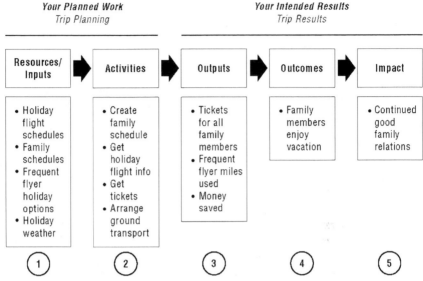

Figure 3.1   Illustrative Example of a Logic Model

for ways that a family vacation would help strengthen those ties. In logic-modeling parlance, the arrows between boxes represent causation. In other words, getting tickets for everyone and saving money *causes* family members to enjoy their vacation. (Hmmm ... We are not convinced this logic model describes every family vacation we've ever taken!) The problem surfaces when those arrows, the linkages, don't work as expected. We can think of our own vacations, where we purchased tickets and saved a great deal of money yet didn't have a great time. But abandoning the model as faulty (trip planning doesn't work!) doesn't feel like the right approach.

This type of evaluation-focused logic model does not encourage or support adaptation in education systems and programs, but it is not intended to do that. Monitoring outputs and outcomes doesn't help us learn and improve our craft as educators. This type of logic model *is* helpful in evaluating and monitoring the fidelity of implementation (FOI) of a program. It is designed to be static so that we can measure the program goals as planned and test out our theory of action (saving money leads to fun family times!). Logic models describe what you expect will happen as a result of what you do. Logic models for evaluative or FOI measurement purposes are not designed to allow for going back and fiddling with or adjusting the key components and elements.

Let's deconstruct an actual logic model (figure 3.2). Suppose a district curriculum development team is developing an early elementary school science program in order to increase students' academic outcomes in

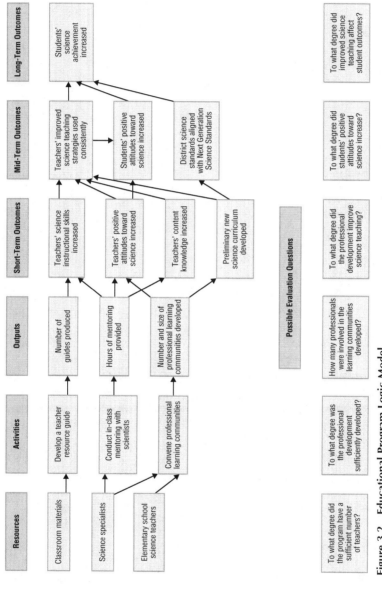

Figure 3.2   Educational Program Logic Model

science (Kekahio, Cicchinelli, Lawton, & Brandon, 2014; Lawton, Brandon, Cicchinelli, & Kekahio, 2014).

This logic model is not going to provide much prescriptive help or direction to the people charged with doing the work or to people who want to replicate a past success. The model tells us, for example, that producing guides will lead to better teaching, which in turn will lead to improved student learning. But it does not indicate or explain what they are doing to achieve all these ambitious outputs and outcomes. This logic model does not answer the most critical question for educators: What are you going to actually do?

We know from research, experience, and many evaluations of educational programs that the pedagogy and policies that do improve teacher effectiveness and student learning are a bit more complex. Developing guides and providing mentoring by real scientists for teachers are not going to cause changing practices by themselves. The model does not specify why and how these guides will lead to an increase in the teachers' science instructional skills. In fact, the model is silent on how the guides will be used at all. While logic models can be a great resource for evaluators to help monitor various outputs and outcomes, they typically lack the information needed to promote and sustain school improvement. Logic models do not provide a way to document and test adaptations to models driven by real-world needs. They are snapshots of practice and are not designed to work with evolving programs. In other words, they do not provide a map to guide either scaling up or scaling down implementations. They are more akin to a picture of a mountain than a trail map.

An alternative to a logic model, focused for and on AI, is the Design and Action Plan (DAP) (see figure 3.3). Rather than having a long series of outputs and outcomes typical of an evaluator's logic model, notice that the DAP focuses on specifying and codifying the key components of the program. It answers the question of this step: *What are we going to do?*

In this Project ExcEL example, the DAP includes the resources (from step 2) in the left column with waypoints and core goal (from step 1) in the right column. The middle column features the key components of the plan. From this DAP, we can see that Project ExcEL features a collaborative approach that includes school districts, program developers, and community partner organizations. These three groups help to implement the key components of the work.

Rather than having column after column of outputs and outcomes, as with a traditional logic model intended for evaluation, the DAP shows the key mediators (immediate outcomes or outputs) and the long-term outcomes. In the AI language, key mediators are the waypoints we described in step 1, and outcomes are the core project goals. The benefit of creating the DAP is that it offers a visual representation of a complex series of programs and supports, drawing them together in a unified road map for all stakeholders to understand, weigh in on, and ultimately rally around. We can keep our "eyes on the prize," if you will, with the mediators/outputs and outcomes. We finally have a clear guide for our journey (textbox 3.1).

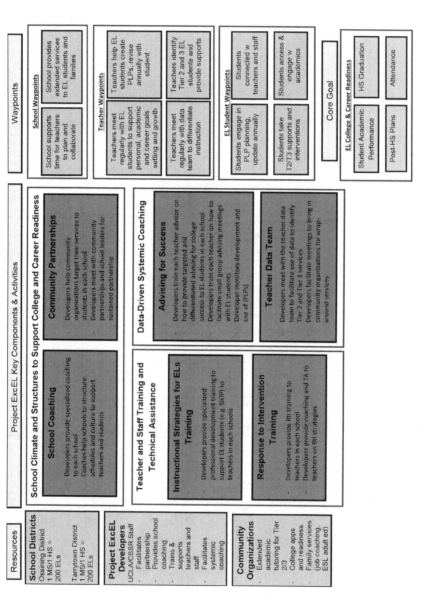

Figure 3.3   Design and Action Plan of Project ExcEL. CSSR: Centre for Social Science Research, EL: English Learner, PLPs: Personalized Learning Plans, Project ExcEL: Project Excellence for English Learners, RtI: Response to Intervention, UCLA: University of California, Los Angeles

---

Textbox 3.1 Adaptive Implementation Team

The AI team works together to brainstorm activities and complete a PCA. They select activities for implementation, determine relationships and synergies, and construct a process road map. The school coach, technical assistance provider, or data expert can facilitate the team meeting.

Process for Developing the Design and Action Plan

Creating your DAP, your detailed road map, is going to take some time. You should also plan on revisiting the DAP each time you reengage with an AI cycle. Remember, the DAP is designed to be flexible, evolving as you learn more about your program during implementation. It would be highly unusual to "get it right" the first time. In fact, when your DAP stops changing, it is a signal that you are no longer learning about the implementation of your program.

You can begin by penciling in your waypoint(s) and core goal(s) in the right-hand column. You've already discussed and set them in step 1, so you know where you are headed. Then you can move over to the left-hand column and write down your resources, the things that will support your journey, identified in step 2.

To design the key components section (activities) of the DAP, start with your PCA to review the list of activities you decided to undertake. The DAP takes the individual activities outlined in the PCA and designs a singular unified action plan wherein the individual activities work together, and completing this middle section of your plan is culmination of this step. The AI team identifies and groups activities selected during the PCA process and determines the relationships and synergies between them. Activities are then mapped out in the center portion of the DAP. Even though this map is built collaboratively, it is very helpful to conduct a series of face-to-face validity meetings with stakeholders *before* you begin implementation. But know at the outset that you are going to revise, revise, and revise again! Recalling our design engineering process, we are always developing the best map for the moment, not the perfect answer or tool for all time.

Identify the Group of Activities Using the Pro and Con Assessment

The PCA is the first step in assessing the list of activities and how they can work together to leverage the strengths of each. From the pro-and-con list, select the activities that meet most of your criteria and seem the most likely to help you reach your waypoint. It might be tempting to select all of the activities, but given the various constraints, this usually is not the best option. Selecting the activities heavily weighted on the pro side (with few challenges) may not be the best choice either. Sometimes, the easiest-to-implement solutions don't give you much in terms of impact. You selected a waypoint that you knew would take effort and learning to reach, so you should *embrace* the opportunity to tackle the challenges it represents. Don't avoid them!

Another way of conceptualizing *how many* activities is to think of the activities as rocks and pebbles in a jar. The jar represents your challenges; you can only do things that fit into the jar. If you start with the small and easy activities (your pebbles) you won't have any room left to fit the bigger, higher-payoff activities (the rocks) into your jar. Again, using a collaborative team can help you prioritize and focus on the "bigger" or more impactful activities. In the PCA list, sort out the activities that will give you the most bang for your buck.

Determine the Relationships and Synergies of Activities

Once you have selected the activities, start thinking through the set as a unified whole or program by looking at the relationships and synergies across and between the activities. How do they work together so that each activity is not a stand-alone activity? Can they be tweaked or further refined so that they work in concert more effectively? Can roles and responsibilities be effectively aligned to build on individual strengths? Considering these factors is essentially reflecting on and building on how different people work together—from the school principal, teachers, and support staff to external partner organizations. How are all of these players and their expertise going to come together and work together?

Map Out the Activities

Once you and your team have a clear idea of the main activities and the relationships between them, map them out. You can do it by hand (e.g., drawing on a white board, chart paper, or digital board), or you can design the map online.

A group process that helps to map out the activities is using self-adhesive notes in different colors; this also offers individuals a chance to review the progress of the mapping and adjust it over time (figure 3.4). Start by writing down your core goal(s) on yellow self-adhesive notes and place them on the far right side of the wall or table. Then write down

Figure 3.4   Placement of Resources, Waypoints, and Core Goal

the waypoints and resources on the light-blue self-adhesive notes. The resources should be on the far left side of the wall or table. The waypoints should be either on top or to the left of the yellow core goal(s) (similar to a logic-model format with columns and columns of outputs and outcomes).

Before moving on to the dark-blue self-adhesive notes to represent the activities, just take a moment to see what you have. Does it make sense? Did you miss an input or an outcome? Does it all hang together as a coherent set of interrelated outputs and outcomes? If not, this is the time to adjust and adapt the model. Since these are just in self-adhesive note form, move the notes around, add to them, or remove some. As you do this, do you see relationships changing? Do you see new connections and synergies coming together and old connections being broken? We find that by doing a big-picture review, we can start seeing and understanding connections more readily.

Once you feel that the inputs, outputs, and outcomes are on target and make conceptual and logical sense, use the dark-blue self-adhesive notes to write down one activity per note and place them in the middle of the wall or table (figure 3.5).

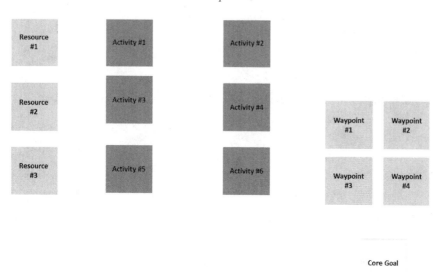

Figure 3.5   Placement of Initial Set of Activities

From our experiences going through the DAP with schools, districts, non-profits, and foundations, there are always ways to make connections so that they work together as a coherent set of activities. When looking for connections, think about who will lead the activities (e.g., school or district staff, an external developer, or a community partner), who the recipients are, when the activities will take place, and where they will take place. Then start grouping and regrouping as you think about how to make the DAP as parsimonious as possible. Again, once you make the connections, take a step back to review the whole model to make sure it still makes conceptual and logical sense (figure 3.6).

Conduct a Series of Face Validity Meetings with Stakeholders

Once you have the DAP, transfer the model to a one-page document (similar to the Project ExcEL figure). This will be used to check for face validity (the "sniff test") with various stakeholders. We recommend—at minimum—meeting with each of the responsible parties that would lead activities (dark-blue self-adhesive notes). Different stakeholders who have been involved in developing the DAP will be responsible for sharing the plan with their peer group. For instance, teachers share with other teachers, principals with other principals, and community organizations with other community organizations. With each meeting, you are obtaining additional feedback to refine and

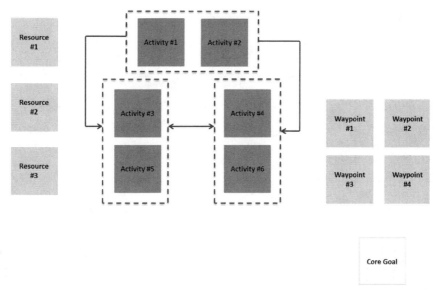

Figure 3.6 Making Connections with Activities

improve your DAP. In so doing, you are also obtaining buy-in for the DAP and ultimately the planned intervention.

Though it can be more work upfront, it is typically more efficient to have separate meetings with each stakeholder group. We often see a stakeholder meeting that includes school and district staff, community members, and parents trying to discuss strategic district plans. This is not an effective strategy to obtain feedback to improve the DAP. Though these larger group meetings may be ideal to disseminate information or present the DAP, this is not the purpose of this phase. Face validity meetings take place to obtain critical feedback to improve your plan. To do so, we recommend separate meetings with no more than five to ten people per stakeholder session to review and provide feedback to improve your plan.

Be careful and thoughtful here when handling suggestions that make your model more complex. The focus in this step of the DAP creation is on improvement and refinement, *not* expansion to integrate every opinion, desire, or wish. Are the changes improving the DAP so that it is easier to implement to achieve the results you seek? If not, resist the urge to add it into your plan, or at least review it once more with the AI team to see if it does indeed add value to your program. In general, we create plans that are too ambitious, so keeping the number of activities to a minimum will help you move toward success.

Revise, Revise, and Revise Again

With each stakeholder meeting, you will be revising the DAP. As noted earlier, this revision process could take multiple iterations, with multiple tweaks or even a complete reconceptualization. The key is to stick with it. As the old adage states, "nothing worth doing is easy."

Just like the engineering process, creating the DAP is not a one-and-done type of process (IDEO, 2012). At the same time, it is important to know when it is "good enough" to implement and test out, so don't let perfect be the enemy of good. You will need to resist the urge to tweak and perfect at every step with the hope of iterating or designing only once.

When you are designing a program, the best design is the one that will meet most of the key needs of stakeholders. Notice, this is not all of the needs of stakeholders. You are working toward consensus, the situation where every stakeholder can live with the plan and agree to test it out to improve it. When you work with groups, don't try to get everyone in the room to agree. Remind your stakeholders that you are testing your first iteration so that you can improve on it. This is the AI mindset!

Is there a sweet spot in the number of iterations and revisions? Of course, the answer is no; it always depends on the context. That said, let's look at the realities of the education space. We have a nine-month calendar schedule to implement something during the school year, we only have students for about 180 days of those months, and we have an annual budget to allocate and plan (usually by April of the previous school year). Timing is of the essence, so be cautious not to get stuck on this step at the expense of doing something.

PROJECT ExcEL EXAMPLE

The Project ExcEL sites in New York started developing the DAP when the project was designed in 2013. Logic models have been a required piece of i3 proposals since the inception of this grant program, and they are now universally expected elements for funding proposals. The United States Department of Education defines logic models as "a reasonable conceptual framework that identifies key components of the proposed project (*i.e.,* the active 'ingredients' that are hypothesized to be critical to achieving the relevant outcomes) and describes the theoretical and operational relationships among the key components and outcomes" (US Department of Education, 2017).

Our ExcEL logic model hypothesized the critical elements, reflecting our thinking and planning in 2013. The unspoken assumption in this approach is

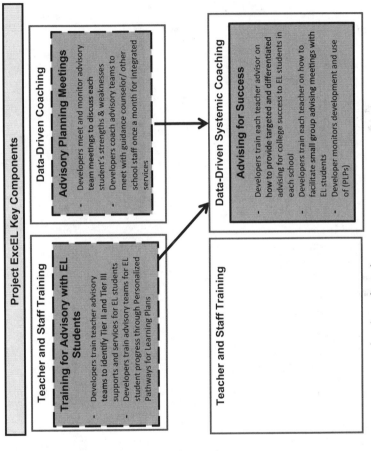

Project ExcEL Key Components

Teacher and Staff Training

Data-Driven Coaching

Advisory Planning Meetings

- Developers meet and monitor advisory team meetings to discuss each student's strengths & weaknesses
- Developers coach advisory teams to meet with guidance counselor/ other school staff once a month for integrated services

Training for Advisory with EL Students

- Developers train teacher advisory teams to identify Tier II and Tier III supports and services for EL students
- Developers train advisory teams for EL student progress through Personalized Pathways for Learning Plans

Data-Driven Systemic Coaching

Advising for Success

- Developers train each teacher advisor on how to provide targeted and differentiated advising for college success to EL students in each school
- Developers train each teacher on how to facilitate small group advising meetings with EL students
- Developer monitors development and use of (PLPs)

Teacher and Staff Training

Figure 3.7   ExcEL DAP Showing Adaptation

that you know, in advance, how the program will work. The program is ultimately measured by judging those assumptions, and only programs that have
been implemented as designed and can demonstrate an impact are deemed
successful. But what happens when you learn and adapt along the way and
your conceptual model shifts? That is what happened during this development phase of ExcEL.

ExcEL's DAP has gone through twelve revisions as of this writing, and
it will continue to evolve. Some of the changes are minor, but others reflect
major redirections in how the program works. One major shift reflected in the
DAP relates to the role of project coaches (figure 3.7).

The original ExcEL DAP (the proposal logic model) discussed three main
components designed to address school climate and culture, teacher and staff
training, and data-driven coaching. These three components integrate to produce changes in schools, teachers, and students (mediators/waypoints). The
program developers originally envisioned providing teacher and staff training in two discrete silos, instructional strategies (teacher and staff training)
and tiering or data use strategies (data-driven coaching). A student advisory
program would be a third silo.

In practice, the kickoff professional development event made this distinction operational by devoting separate days (and experts) to each topic.
As we moved deeper into the process and school-based teams began
meeting regularly, it quickly became apparent that instruction, data use,
and advising were integrated and used seamlessly by the people doing
the work.

In retrospect, this may seem obvious—teaching is not silos of information
but the craft of integrating various pedagogical knowledge and theories with
engaging curriculum and materials. A mistake would have been to keep the
original DAP as is and push to change teacher behavior. Instead, we adapted
and the team meetings became the time and place to accomplish all these
activities with the support of a single coaching team. The data-driven systemic coaching section of our DAP was born. We revised the DAP with each
iteration and learning.

The conversation between ExcEL evaluators and program developers that
led to this revision was an underlying force in promoting our own thinking
about the AI process. Leading the way in this case, the practitioners (the
people doing the work) simply modified the process to make it work in their
context. We discovered during the first year of implementation that our program design had to deviate from our original proposal (our logic model) to
become successful.

Step 4

What Did We Do?

There is probably a long period of time elapsing between step 3, when you started on your journey of planning what to do, and step 4, when you pause, reflect, and document what you actually did. You are at or close to your waypoint, so you stop and look over your shoulder to check out the ground you have covered; or, you are hopelessly lost, so stopping and looking back will give you the chance to backtrack and try again.

Your Design and Action Plan (DAP) provided the road map for your team, describing the activities you planned to do as you moved toward your waypoint. But were these activities actually implemented? Was your timeline accurate? Did you have the resources you thought you did? The gap between what you planned and what you did represents the very core of adaptive implementation thinking. There's no right or wrong here, only reflection on the DAP and your data.

Navigators refer to a process known as "terrain association," where they compare their anticipated route to conditions on the ground. They will stop and pull out their map or plan and mentally retrace the most recent leg of the journey. Perhaps one stretch was too slippery to navigate because of icy conditions, so they ended up bypassing it and finding a way around it. Or maybe they stumbled onto a previously unmarked trail that saved lots of time and effort. Whatever they discovered, this is the time to associate their plan with their actions and make notes to inform the people that follow them along this route. This is the time to annotate the road map.

ANNOTATE YOUR ROAD MAP

Some journeys are longer than others, and to support the Adaptive Implementation (AI) team's reflection process you need a process to capture and document your actions along the way. Not only does this improve recall, but it also provides you with a more accurate retelling by capturing small, ongoing adaptations that you might overlook when you reflect on the big picture. You can accomplish this with a systematic, individual journaling process. Having one team member oversee the process, remind everyone to keep up, and organize the notes streamlines this process.

This ongoing journaling process is not just an organizational aid. There are frequent "on the fly" changes and adaptations made all the time during implementation that are forgotten or never repeated. Have you ever had to adapt a recipe right in the middle of dinner service? Maybe you forgot to add seasoning to the taco fillings, so you grab your spices and put them on the table. Now everyone can season their dinner to their individual taste. That's an adaptation to your process and maybe one you want to record and remember. You could make a note directly on your recipe card right after dinner so you don't forget about it (textbox 4.1).

Textbox 4.1 Adaptive Implementation Team

The AI team works together to create a description of activities as implemented. They use formative data to decide how close they are to their designated waypoint. The data expert is ideal for the role of journaling the process.

These on-the-fly changes, where people interact with reality and make adjustments, are exactly the type of responses AI is designed to capture. This is where you can capture the professional knowledge and wisdom that emerges during program implementation. Duffy (2003) found "that systemic change is sometimes serpentine, sometimes circular, and sometimes spiral, but never purely linear and sequential" (p. 36).

It is during this stage of adjustment that momentum needs to keep building to avoid a return to old habits and ways of doing things. In this momentum, we are busy doing the work. It will become very tempting to stop documenting the process. After all, we are all busy implementing and doing the work, not taking notes. But because systemic change is often not linear, with adaptations being made at large and small scales, documenting what was done is of the utmost importance. This is why designating the one team member to document the process will help in the AI process.

WHAT TO ANNOTATE AND DOCUMENT?

Having a road map (DAP) to get you started on an intended path is necessary, but you have to be willing to examine new information, perspectives, and outcomes on the way that may result in a few detours along your route. You need to associate your terrain. The annotation of the DAP is the narrative of your journey, and it highlights adaptations and learning and informs your next steps. They leave a rich, detailed map for others to follow.

In this step, you will use formative assessment processes to reflect on the journey, using information and data collected along the way. Thacker, Bell, and Schargel (2009) remind us that "assessment is not a 'find a problem and fix it' process" (p. 45) but rather a process geared toward improvement. In AI, we focus on more immediate formative information sources. Schools are extremely data-rich environments, with lots of different types of data available. The collective information should allow you to see if you have arrived at your waypoint.

To determine what information to collect and use, we recommend using the DAP as the framework. The DAP provides the list of activities and intended waypoint(s). For each of these items in the DAP, create a crosswalk that links the needed information, data, and measures. Instead of creating a whole new set of data collection activities to fit the DAP, we strongly suggest starting with what you already have. The trick is to figure out how to access existing information and repurpose it to demonstrate progress toward your core goal.

For example, rather than creating a teacher survey to determine the value of the training, during the next staff meeting, do a quick show of hands to ask these questions. Instead of creating a student test on math strategies, collect student work that shows their thought process and work. Rather than conducting focus groups of parents to see if they are reading to their children, go to a parent–teacher conference or Back-to-School night to do a show of hands to ask these questions. Instead of creating a student engagement survey to determine if students are more engaged in class, ask other teachers to confirm your own observations on student engagement. Rather than create an observation protocol of teacher effectiveness, ask teachers during the next staff meeting to reflect on what worked and what they would do to improve instruction.

The process for gathering the information and making it available for the AI team discussion needs to be explicit or it won't happen. The team must decide what information will be used, who will collect it, how it will be collected, and when it will be available. Again, remember that this is a collaborative process, and everyone has a role in gathering the information.

A helpful tool in annotating and documenting information related to the DAP is the data review sheet (table 4.1). The data review sheet starts with the waypoint right at the top. Each row is an activity from the DAP with an honest assessment of how it was implemented, with notes.

Table 4.1   Data Review Sheet Template

Waypoint: Write in the Waypoint(s) from Your DAP

Activities and Key Components	Yes/All of the Time	No/Some of the Time	No/Not at All	Notes
Activity 1: Each row represents an activity (box) from the DAP	Check if AI team agrees this was done.	Check if AI team agrees this was not done well or only sometimes done.	Check if AI team agrees this was not done at all.	AI team scribe annotates and documents information from data gathered by all members of the AI team, paying particular attention to what was not done but adapted.
Activity 2: Each row represents an activity (box) from the DAP	Check if AI team agrees this was done.	Check if AI team agrees this was not done well or only sometimes done.	Check if AI team agrees this was not done at all.	AI team scribe annotates and documents information from data gathered by all members of the AI team, paying particular attention to what was not done but adapted.
Activity 3: Each row represents an activity (box) from the DAP	Check if AI team agrees this was done.	Check if AI team agrees this was not done well or only sometimes done.	Check if AI team agrees this was not done at all.	AI team scribe annotates and documents information from data gathered by all members of the AI team, paying particular attention to what was not done but adapted.

AI: Adaptive Implementation, DAP: Design and Action Plan

The AI team will look at the gap(s) between what you planned to do and what you actually did and use evidence, information collected, and professional knowledge to decide if you have hit your waypoint. Looking and sifting through all of this information and knowledge is not a solitary exercise. Rather, it is a robust, collaborative process with the AI team members to annotate and describe the journey. The ensuing discussions shape your next steps, what you learned from doing, and leave an enhanced road map for the teams that follow you.

ANNOTATING IS NOT EVALUATING

It is important to be upfront about this step. This is not a teacher performance evaluation to determine which teacher should get a bonus. This is not a project evaluation to determine what project to fund. The AI process is to keep improving our craft of teaching. Therefore, there is value in being transparent and honest about the assessment of whether an activity was done all, some, or none of the time. There is much learning to be gleaned when something is not done. From annotating and documenting, we learn that something else (that could be better) was done instead.

This step begins the "growth mindset" (Dweck, 2006) mentality among the AI team. The focus is on mastery of tasks, not the sheer performance of tasks promoting a competitive environment (Maehr & Midgley, 1996) among AI team members. On the contrary, this step is really about synthesizing data and information and should be a judgment-free zone.

PROJECT ExcEL EXAMPLE

Let's take the example of the ExcEL team's statement, *We need to see more effective instruction in our classrooms.* The team's initial road map was fairly straightforward and included providing professional development, followed by coaching to support implementation. Pretty straightforward. In reality, the path we traveled looked very different. Nearly half the teachers involved were not available for training in August, and finding time to meet as a whole team was challenging for different reasons at each site. The skill and knowledge levels of team members varied widely. In the end, we adapted by providing, leaning more heavily on collaborative coaching and less on traditional professional development.

Clearly, describing the path we took is important, but we need to see where we are as well! We might be at our intended stopping point, but we might also be lost in the woods. We might have stumbled into a much better stopping point with the potential to shorten or strengthen our journey. When we identified our waypoint in step 1, we framed it in terms of *what I need to see*. We described our waypoint as a specific, observable measure. Where we are and whether or not we hit our waypoint is an important, explicit piece of the story that needs to be told in this step.

At the end of the first year of ExcEL implementation, our team paused to reflect on implementation. One of the mechanisms we used was a simple checklist. In the left-hand column, we listed the activities we planned to do, based on our DAP.

These sheets were completed during team meetings, capturing the "reality" from multiple perspectives (table 4.2). The middle columns indicate a quick

Table 4.2 ExcEL Data Review Sheet

Waypoint: We Need to See Improved Instruction for ELs in Our Classrooms

Activities and Key Components	Yes/All of the Time	No/Some of the Time	No/Not at All	Notes
School coach conducts one needs assessment at each school	X			Coach revised needs assessment mid-year. Needs assessment not integrated and communicated with whole school staff.
Five (5) coaching sessions are provided at each school per year		X		Some schools had more than five sessions, while others had three due to scheduling conflicts at the school. Hard to coordinate scheduling.
School supports time for teachers to plan and collaborate		X		Some schools have AI planning team or teacher data team. This is working well and should be kept.
Teachers meet regularly with EL students to support personal, academic, and career goals			X	Teachers meet but not regularly throughout the year, especially content teachers.
Teachers help EL students create PLPs, revise annually with student			X	With emphasis on coteaching, schools have not created PLPs.
Students engage in PLPs, update annually with teacher			X	Students not part of PLP process.
Students connected with teachers and staff		X		Some students are using the after-school services and getting more attention, but we can do better.
Students have access and engage with academics		X		With emphasis on coteaching, EL teachers are coteaching with content teachers, making EL students more engaged in the subject. This should be kept.

ELs: English Learners, PLPs: Personalized Learning Plans

assessment on whether these were accomplished. The last column is a place for notes on what we did, what we did not do, what we changed, and ideas for change or improvement that surfaced. This right-hand column served as the basis for understanding our adaptations.

Remember, this is not a teacher evaluation procedure, or any type of program evaluation. Indicating that something did not happen is a *good* thing in the AI process because this is important information to use for improvement. Transparency and honesty is important in this step; without it, there will be no learning to be had. By making an honest assessment that teachers did not meet with English Learner (EL) students regularly, nor were teachers creating personalized learning plans for EL students, we were able to identify why that was, what was done instead, and what could be done in the next planning cycle.

The data review sheet helps to synthesize the various data with information on what worked, what did not work, what might have worked, and what should change. The team combined this data with the more formal student assessment data (English Language Arts Assessments, Math Benchmark Assessments, and English Language Development Assessments) that is routinely part of the discussion. Taken together, this process helps to collectively review the data to make inferences about the effective pathways to instructional change in the classroom.

Step 5

What Did We Learn?

You've made it to the end of your first Adaptive Implementation (AI) cycle. That means you agreed on your waypoint and navigated your way to it. You *did* something and *evaluated* how well it worked. But what can you learn from the experience?

More traditional evaluation and improvement science approaches focus narrowly on measuring the gap between what you expected and what you achieved (Fixen, Naoom, Blase, Friedman, & Wallace, 2005; Hulleman & Cordray, 2010; Werner, 2004). This is where we use formal or informal analysis to decide if a program worked. The fidelity and outcome grid shows that we use what we have learned about the process and the outcomes to make a final judgment on the program and its potential for replication. This analysis is clearly important and surfaces important data, but it fails to adequately capture what you learned about the program (figure 5.1).

Let's turn our attention to the dinner problem again. We inventoried our groceries and came up with a plan for dinner. We cooked it and served it. We talked about the relative success of this recipe. In short, we've worked through our problem and found a satisfactory solution. But we haven't explicitly thought through what we learned and how we can use that knowledge to improve tomorrow's dinner. We have solved a problem but haven't yet *adapted* the process.

Once you and your family have reached this point in the cycle and understand what you achieved (maybe over dessert), you need to pause and reflect on the process. What have you learned about the dinner-making process, and how can you be better prepared the next time it occurs?

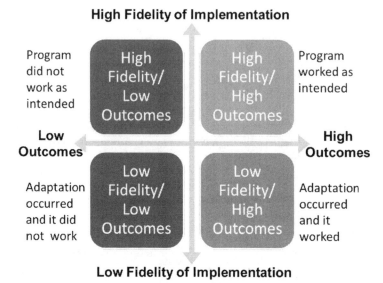

High Fidelity of Implementation

Program did not work as intended — High Fidelity/ Low Outcomes — High Fidelity/ High Outcomes — Program worked as intended

Low Outcomes ← → **High Outcomes**

Adaptation occurred and it did not work — Low Fidelity/ Low Outcomes — Low Fidelity/ High Outcomes — Adaptation occurred and it worked

Low Fidelity of Implementation

Figure 5.1   Implementation and Outcome Grid

WILL WE DO IT AGAIN?

Not every program or plan requires continuous adjustment or attention, and very few require it forever. In the case of providing a quick, healthy dinner you know you will be in the same situation again, probably soon. Your learning from this cycle might result in restocking the freezer to increase the ingredients you have on hand next time—and another trip around the AI cycle will help you determine what to keep on your weekly grocery list. Your Design and Action Plan (DAP) for providing a quick dinner might approach perfection—you know how to do this! Until, of course, your teenager walks in and unexpectedly announces that she has turned vegetarian. Time to start your planning over.

In educational settings, it is perfectly appropriate to stop and ask if you want to continue with the work you have started, and that is a worthwhile question whether or not you got the results you expected. Sometimes you try a process or program and you end up opting to walk away from it— though only after a deep learning discussion that ensures you don't abandon an effort simply because it is difficult or it did not result in the expected outcome.

At the other end of the spectrum, you may decide that the process is as good and worthwhile as it will get for now, and while you opt to continue the program you no longer need to intentionally adapt and improve the process.

You have implemented and measured the program's impact. You are pleased with the results and plan to continue the work as is. You may decide to reengage in the AI cycle to expand your program (scaling up approach) or to create a better fit within your local context (scaling down approach).

"Continuous improvement" is an all-encompassing approach that is sometimes erroneously applied to everything around us. The approach systematically seeks small, incremental improvements that improve the overall outcome. When you decide to reengage for continuous improvement, you see promise in the results of the initial cycle and believe minor modifications will make the next iteration stronger. Continuous improvement in a district-wide professional development program might mean shifting the delivery mechanism to a web-based experience, allowing more teachers to participate.

This *what have we learned?* step requires you and your team to think through the reasons for continuing, and continuing to adapt, any process or program. Just as you don't want to abandon program implementation simply because it is difficult, you also don't want to endlessly tinker with programs unless you are sure you need to continue to improve your process.

WHEN WE DO IT AGAIN ...

You might be asking yourself right now if this process ever ends! As educators, we face new challenges every day because our students change as they mature and develop, and every day brings us new students with new stories. Change and adaptation in education never ends, and the AI process is designed to accompany, structure, and reinvigorate our practice by helping to streamline and focus improvement efforts. AI also helps teachers and school leaders gird against constant policy shifts, district- or state-level leadership changes and the requisite changes that accompany them, professional development carte du jour, and a host of other features of the shifting education landscape. We slow things down, we reflect, and we adapt with intention.

These learning conversations will be guided by your program's DAP, which lays out the logical sequence of events you expect to see unfold and helps you tie your process to your impact. The use of the DAP in this learning step underscores a key difference between a fidelity of implementation (FOI) approach and an "AI" approach.

Under the FOI model, the DAP is an inflexible model framework that we strive to implement as described. The tacit understanding is that, if implemented correctly, the model will yield the desired results. Under the AI model, the DAP is a fluid framework that we strive to test, adapt, and strengthen. The tacit understanding is that we do not (yet) understand the elements of success in our context, and we need to experiment and adapt the model to reach the desired results.

SCALING UP

Scaling up is about adapting your program to fit a wider audience. Piloting a program on a small scale before widespread implementation is a common example of scaling up. AI is an important tool to use in developing programs for replication and "scaling up," even though that is not its sole purpose. As programs are piloted and tested, we can learn a great deal about what works in each context, capturing that information and using it to refine elements of any model. Figure 5.2 shows how AI cycles can be used to document and improve a replicable model.

At the end of one cycle, we discern necessary adaptations that should be tried in the next round. Trailblazers, whether on a mountain or in a district education office, are piloting the first iteration of an AI cycle. They create their waypoint, pack their bags, and get going! But they pause to reflect, associate the terrain, and update their maps. As they move on in their own journey,

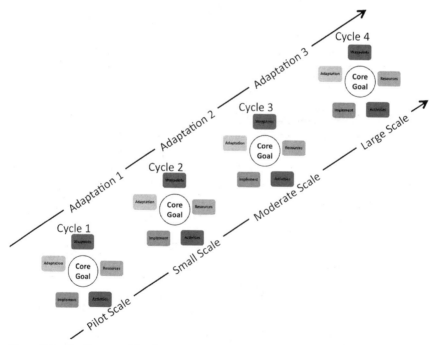

Figure 5.2   Scaling up with Adaptive Implementation

they leave a better map behind for others to follow. This makes successive replications simpler and more effective.

SCALING DOWN

When you learn and adapt your program, trying for a better fit in the same site, you are scaling down. "Scaling down" has been introduced as a concept unique to AI, and it is especially germane at this learning step. The impetus to adopt evidence-based programming and best practice continues to grow, with little attention paid to adapting these programs to fit the local implementation culture. Reengagement for scaling down purposes is an important alternative to abandoning the program for lack of a strong fit; it explicitly acknowledges the need for adaptation. Scaling down an evidence-based program might mean thoughtful melding of new curricula with locally developed materials, creating a unique instructional guide that builds on existing strengths and practices, or taking advantage of key personnel or a cohort of students to adapt practices and materials to fill a potential need.

LEARNING THROUGH REFLECTION

This learning step requires a thoughtful and focused collaborative discussion to result in meaningful learning and a plan for moving forward. Learning reflections are key components of establishing a data-driven culture in schools, and most educators have experience in using conversational protocols. While there are many ways to structure this conversation, using a protocol ensures that every team member has the opportunity to share their insights and the team can strategize based on consideration of all the available evidence.

In just one iteration, a lot happened! You focused on a waypoint, figured out constraints and resources, outlined the set of activities in your action plan, did the work, and analyzed the results. There is a lot of data to reflect upon, and you are using that data to decide if you will continue to iterate and what you will do differently. In analyzing what you learned, you will think through the following questions:

- What resources were used?
- What did we plan to do?
- What did we actually do?
- What worked?
- How do we know it worked?

Textbox 5.1 Adaptive Implementation Team

The AI team holds a debrief meeting to discuss what worked, what didn't, and lessons for the next iteration. The team uses formative data as a start-off point to plan ahead. The school coach, technical assistance provider, or data expert is ideal to facilitate this meeting.

These questions should sound familiar. These are the foundation or building blocks of the AI process. Teachers adapt materials, curriculum, and instructional approaches all the time, even without explicit awareness. Just like good chefs who rarely follow recipes, good teachers rarely follow curriculum verbatim! The best part about this step—the learning step—is that you get to actively design adaptations to your process or program. You and your team strategize what you will do differently next time (textbox 5.1).

Using the AI model and tools will provide a tremendous amount of data showing what we did, what worked, what did not, and why (figure 5.3). When we deviate from the recipe, there will be documentation of where we broke with the plan and why. When and why did your professional knowledge steer you in another direction? If we do it all again, will it be just as effective? What will make it more effective? And possibly the most important question: If things did not work out, is it because of what we were unable to implement properly, or is ours simply not a program worth pursuing?

Teams can (and should) use whatever collaborative process and protocol they are comfortable with, as long as the conversation is facilitated,

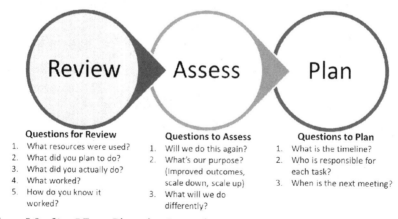

Questions for Review
1. What resources were used?
2. What did you plan to do?
3. What did you actually do?
4. What worked?
5. How do you know it worked?

Questions to Assess
1. Will we do this again?
2. What's our purpose? (Improved outcomes, scale down, scale up)
3. What will we do differently?

Questions to Plan
1. What is the timeline?
2. Who is responsible for each task?
3. When is the next meeting?

Figure 5.3   Step 5 Team Discussion Protocol

focused, and honors all voices. This is not a conversation that can be rushed, and it may take more than one session to fully explore each question. Making the time to thoroughly explore these questions will be worth it in the long run.

Team members should have all the materials from the earlier steps available, and the team facilitator should take time to chart and review the findings from steps 1 through 4. This helps ground the discussion in the just completed cycle and ensures that the conversation is evidence-based. The facilitator then structures a process to consider these three questions:

- Will we do this again?
- What's our purpose? (Improve the outcomes, scale down, scale up.)
- What will we do differently?

It is imperative to leave with a clear plan for the next program iteration that includes next steps and timelines.

AI truly is a part of good teaching and good schools. Effective educators reflect, learn, adapt, and cycle through again. As educators, we must be wary of anyone who professes that they have a working turnkey model guaranteed to produce results. There is no program, no activity, no style of teaching that we can implement, press cruise control or engage autopilot, and then sit back and watch success bubble forth.

Navigating your way through the school-reform landscape is always challenging. If it was easy, we would have figured out all the answers a long time ago. The philosophy guiding how we think about improvement has swung dramatically from "I know it when I see it" to "without a randomized control study we really don't know anything about its effectiveness." AI pulls the best from each of these worlds and charts a course right down the middle. Research and professional knowledge are best applied together.

PROJECT ExcEL EXAMPLE

Project ExcEL's core goal is to improve the college readiness of English Learner (EL) students. To achieve this core goal, one of the waypoints is to enhance the instructional capacity of mainstream teachers working with ELs, operationalized primarily through a summer professional development experience coupled with onsite coaching to support implementation. The content of the professional development was intentionally left open-ended, recognizing the changing needs of the students and teachers. Planning for the summer institute format and focus is done each spring by a team of teachers and administrators working with the project developers.

During the second project year, research began to emerge on *language learning progressions*. Language progressions provide tools to help teachers accurately assess their student's developmental level and differentiate instruction appropriately. The summer institute planning team discussed language progressions and opted to make it the content focus of professional development during the 2016 summer institute. An expert was provided for two days of training along with associated materials and resources. Yet midway through the 2016–2017 school year, not a single teacher was using the language progressions in any way in their classrooms.

Without the AI cycle, one would think language progressions do not work and we should get rid of it. Instead, the ExcEL leadership team (our project AI team) looked at the implementation of language progressions as part of an AI cycle. Over the course of ninety minutes, the team worked through the first five questions in the AI Discussion Protocol: What resources were used? What did you plan to do? What did you actually do? What worked? How do you know it worked?

In going through the discussion protocol questions, this example shows when something does not work. Even with summer training, ongoing planning meetings, and school coaching, we discovered that no one was implementing language progressions in their classroom. A critical piece of information was why? During this discussion, it became clear that we lacked a shared understanding of what language progressions are and how they can be used to support instructional change and improvement in the classroom. We used this discovery to guide our learning step and planning for the next iteration—*we want to learn more about language progressions and need additional time to build a deeper understanding on the part of the teachers.*

In this instance, we decided to move forward with another iteration in order to improve the process and results. The next iteration will do some things differently, starting with the opportunity to study the "big ideas" in more depth before moving directly into implementation. The team left with a plan to create a smaller study group to gather information and present their findings to the AI team in one month's time. We captured the learning discussion in the form of an outline for a new AI cycle that will help us keep the process on track and make sure we don't get derailed by endless study. Our outline followed the AI discussion protocol with the following lessons learned:

- Will we do this again?
- What's our purpose? (Improve the outcomes, scale down, scale up.)
- What will we do differently?

Will we do this again?

- Yes, we will cycle through learning progressions one more time, but we need the following resources:
  - We need the instructional leaders at each school to be cheerleaders for this approach.
  - We need time to build a deeper understanding on the part of the teachers.
  - We need resources to support connections with other schools using the progressions.

What's our purpose?

- We want to see evidence that language progressions can improve classroom practice.

What will we do differently?

- We will identify volunteers interested in creating a study group to develop a plan of action for the leadership team.

Conclusion and Discussion

There is a German proverb: *Was der Kopf macht nicht, die Fuesse muss zweimal tuen* (What the head doesn't do, the feet do twice). This snippet of homespun advice goes to the heart of why Adaptive Implementation (AI) is so critical to educational reform initiatives. AI emerged as a concept from conversations born out of frustration with existing tools and processes designed to monitor program implementation, but not necessarily supportive of improving programs. Negative examples abounded. Fidelity of implementation (FOI) measures imply high scores (good fidelity) are correlated with successful programs (Fixen et al., 2005).

We think high FOI could mean that the program is easy to implement and scale, and it could lead most directly and consistently to improving student outcomes (as the program intends). Similarly, we think poorly of programs with the lowest scores on FOI, where the results could indicate that the program is too cumbersome to implement and could not be replicable at scale. Most importantly, we believe low fidelity scores mean we cannot reliably impact student outcomes. Through elaborate logic models, we carefully create a long list of short-term, moderate-term, and long-term outcomes to track, measure, and assess impacts. Yet these traditional program implementation tools and processes fall short of helping us understand how to improve our model or how to implement research-based models in our own context.

There's nothing wrong with rigorous research and the use of fidelity indices. In fact, they represented a significant step forward in the field of education research when they moved out of the university and into the mainstream with No Child Left Behind (NCLB). But we are applying FOI to answer too many questions. We are using FOI to answer technical questions (did we do what was planned?) as well as adaptive questions (what types of activities work and in what context?).

When in an adaptive system, the strict application of the FOI model has two major limitations in improving teaching and learning (an adaptive and dynamic system). First, the strict FOI model, especially to complex reforms, can result in the conclusion that the model, and its implementation, was seriously flawed. While that may be true in some cases, there is no reasonable way to capture the actions that might have resulted in a very different outcome. This professional knowledge, developed during the implementation process, is overshadowed by the lack of positive findings.

Second, the strict FOI model assumes that a teacher follows a specific recipe (FOI) and has no room for adapting the recipe based on their professional knowledge and assessment of the consumers (the students). But research has consistently shown that effective schools and teaching is an interaction between quality curriculum, instruction (teachers), and students (Ball & Cohen, 1996; Cohen, Raudenbush, & Ball, 2003). Strictly following the intervention as designed does not allow for any improvements and learning.

We showcase two rigorous, well-conducted research studies, almost ten years apart, to highlight how standard implementation and impact studies do little to inform practice. The first is a thorough research study of the Comprehensive School Reform (CSR) model. The second is a national impact study of Response to Intervention (RtI).

In the case of CSR models, research from RAND Education concluded that the mixed results in student outcomes were often due to a lack of proper implementation (Vernez et al., 2006). However, there has not been an in-depth examination of why implementation was not done properly, nor whether it should have been done in the first place. The RAND study found that implementation was heavily influenced by the level of teacher preparation, the amount of training provided beforehand, staff commitment to the program, and ongoing support. Additional important conclusions from the study include the fact that schools were clearly favoring certain aspects of the model over others and were intentionally choosing to leave out anything that was found to be unnecessary or a hindrance. In fact, only a miniscule number of the schools in the study actually implemented all aspects of the CSR models. The study recommended further research into the effectiveness of specific practices embedded in the models, rather than the overall model.

Consider how the conclusions of this study might have been improved in both depth and applicability in the field if an AI study had been conducted. We might have developed a deeper understanding of why teachers picked some elements over others for implementation and what the differential effects of those choices were. Without an AI study component, the opportunity to explore ways in which administrators resolve and implement competing initiatives in their building is lost and may lead to repeated attempts at implementation in situations that are doomed to repeated failures.

In the case of RtI, Balu and her colleagues (2015) found that among the 119 elementary schools in the study, 86 percent showed "full implementation" of the RtI framework in grades 1–3 in reading. These schools used a reading screening test taken in the fall to group students into Tier 1, Tier 2, and Tier 3 groups. Based on a fall reading screening test, students who scored just below the reading benchmark were placed in Tier 2 or 3 and were given targeted reading interventions during the school year. Through school surveys, the researchers found that schools were indeed implementing the program by providing more intense small-group instruction and more reading intervention services to Tier 2 and Tier 3 students. In fact, the schools were providing reading interventions to all students (45 percent of schools), as well as targeted reading interventions during core reading instruction time (67 percent of schools).

This information on FOI would suggest that all students should have done better given that these schools were providing more reading services and interventions to students, particularly those students with the most need. However, there were no significant differences in reading outcomes in grades 2–3, and there were negative outcomes for first graders. In essence, when the program was implemented *as designed*, student outcomes were not predictable. Schools participating in the evaluation spent eight years trying to adhere to the program, instead of learning and adapting to fit their own context and the needs of their own students. We are left with very little information except conjecture on what happened or how to improve student outcomes.

Consider how much more we could have learned from this if an AI study had been conducted. This is a case where schools seemed to be implementing a program with high fidelity, and yet it produced negative student outcomes. Rather than eliminating RtI all together, an AI approach would have looked at how students were sorted into the tiers, how each tier provided the differentiated instruction needed, how special education services were identified and provided, and how teachers planned together across the tiers of students.

During the time of these studies, imagine the number of superintendent changes, district and school leadership changes, staffing changes, and even shifts in community labor markets that impact student mobility and attendance (Chingos, Whitehurst, & Lindquist, 2014; Grissom & Andersen, 2012). An AI approach to RtI would have been to cycle through the AI process within one school year; gain insights from students, parents, teachers, and reading coaches; and adapt with each cycle. The focus would have been to use RtI as the set of coordinated activities (the Design and Action Plan [DAP]) to improve student reading, with the DAP providing the road map of school and teacher activities. At the end of the year, we would gather our data on what we did and the impact on student reading scores. We would reflect and see what worked well and what not so well. We would decide if we would continue with RtI, and if so, what adaptations we would make for the next cycle to see more student gains in reading. The AI process is a design engineering approach; we are always thinking about how to improve.

Once you begin thinking about AI, examples pop up all around you. Going all the way back to the hangry teen and the pressure to put dinner on the table, an adaptive parent learned (in step 5) to skip the frozen veggies in the quick taco recipe and next time will put a tastier version on the table. Without AI, quick tacos might disappear from the menu all together since the first try failed to meet the core goal of providing a tasty and nutritious meal. Likewise, we abandon many educational initiatives and reforms when the initial attempts do not move us closer to the goal. We forego the chance to learn and adapt.

TO USE OR NOT TO USE?

While AI is a powerful tool, it is not the hammer to use on everything that looks like a nail! Instead, AI is most useful when you are working within systems characterized by adaptive change. AI is the solution to use to move you closer to the answers in a complicated inquiry. Technical challenges have known solutions; in technical systems, a straightforward approach of implementation with fidelity is the right answer. But with adaptive challenges, the solution is unknown and only an adaptive process will help move you closer to answers.

So, the first question you might ask yourself when selecting an implementation approach is *Do we already know how to accomplish this task and meet our core goals?* Say, for example, you are introducing the use of Carnegie Learning's Cognitive Tutor in your blended learning classrooms. The package is developed, the hardware is in place, and the time frame for student interaction is set. AI is not going to help you in this situation since you already know (or can find out) how to implement the program. This is a situation where FOI is more applicable.

Conversely, if you are tasked with improving English Learner (EL) student Algebra I, AI is an excellent tool to use. Your core goal is clear (it's known), but the solution is unclear (it's unknown). In this instance, AI can help you move closer to an acceptable solution.

A second question to ask yourself when selecting an implementation approach is *Are we genuinely open to change?* That goes far beyond a question about your ability to be flexible—it is much more about an honest look at the constraints already in place. Many implementation programs in education come with implicit or explicit structures that limit the ability to change and adapt, and ultimately to learn. That's also a nice way of asking if you have predetermined outcomes for your group and really aren't flexible enough to reconsider your own assumptions.

The AI process is being used in Project ExcEL to shift ownership from the researchers and program developers to a model of shared leadership with practitioners. This shift has major implications for the research accountability structure and, ultimately, accountability to the funder, in this case ED. The funding was awarded with the understanding that the ExcEL approach (described in a logic model) would be implemented and tested. Our task has been to tease out the fixed elements of the model (the nonnegotiables) from the implementation elements we want to see evolve and adapt.

For example, a key design element of ExcEL is the development of a student-centered, personalized learning culture for EL students at each site. The design concept detailed a number of potential solutions to this problem of practice: flexible scheduling, student advisory, and student-led conferencing. A technical approach would assume that we know these will work, and we simply need to provide the training and support to institute them. But under our adaptive approach, we bring a collaborative team together to learn from what is in place and try out new approaches as we move closer to our solution.

It is just as important to be clear about what is not open to change. Nonnegotiables relate directly to your core goal and are not on the table for discussion by the AI team. In the example above, Project ExcEL's core goal is to improve college readiness of ELs. One specific outcome is to create a student-centered learning culture. The core goal and outcome cannot be altered by the AI process. Being explicit and clear about the nonnegotiables at the outset will prevent the frustrating rehashing of decisions already made and focus energies on improving and moving forward.

WHO'S AT THE TABLE?

Getting the right people involved is crucial to the success of any effort, and AI teams are no different. A core principle underlying the AI is learning from the people doing the work—and that is going to define your team. Having said that, there are AI cycles going on all the time at different levels, "big cycles" and "little cycles" that overlap and interact and generally keep the wheels moving in a forward direction. Everyone doing the work should be involved, but not at every level or every time.

The core goal of getting a nutritious and delicious meal on the table fast has a small, somewhat informal AI team—composed of the people who will be sharing dinner (doing the work). Without the input of the hangry teen, you will not have feedback on the taste (the adaptation), and without the input of the cook, you will not understand what's on hand in the fridge (the resources). "Little" AI cycles like this happen all the time in education, among teachers and even within the classroom. Though they intentionally follow the same steps, they might be characterized by frequent and informal conversations as members "check in" with one another. Sometimes steps are skipped, and sometimes they go in a different order or oscillate between two or three points.

At the other end of the spectrum you find "big" cycles. These are not necessarily more important in terms of impact but are generally seen as more formal. Meetings are planned and the steps are addressed in order and comprehensively. Program implementations calling for "big" AI cycles typically have core goals with a wider impact. But it is important to understand that even the biggest cycle still needs a team comprised of a small group of people doing the work. Once you move away from involving the people doing the work, you are no longer learning and adapting, you are merely directing.

As the management of Project ExcEL evolved, we learned more about who should be at the big and little tables (our process adapts too!). Tellingly, we discovered that securing buy-in and shared leadership is directly related to who sits at the table. Like many other large-scale educational reform projects, ExcEL was conceived by a project design team composed primarily of education researchers and evaluators. While practitioners were consulted and certainly contributed their ideas, it was clear that it was a university-led project. A team of experts listened but ultimately made programmatic decisions. Information flowed out to the teachers and students. Not surprisingly, it often felt like pushing uphill, and uptake was, at best, uneven.

We have evolved our own AI mind-set with the mantra *This is OUR project, not MINE.* While the university researchers clearly have an important role to play in the work, to be successful, leadership needs to be shared with the practitioners and ultimately owned by them.

Deciding who sits at the table and honoring the voice of the people doing the work has a foundational impact on equity within the community. While some of this is implicit in the text, and some is outside the scope, it is important to make explicit mention of it here. We are all familiar with the biblical concept of giving a man a fish and feeding him for a day versus teaching him to fish and feeding him for a lifetime. An AI core precept might be *Parks and Recreation*'s Ron Swanson's thought of "Leave a man alone and he'll figure it out, fishing isn't that hard." This sentiment was also echoed by some of the Project ExcEL teachers. AI honors the knowledge of the people doing the work and represents an important shift in equity. It assumes that you already know how to fish. You just need the time to think, reflect, and improve your craft. This shift in equity occurs when the leadership and knowledge emanates from the practitioners, not necessarily from the researchers, evaluators, or senior administrators.

Shane Mulhern, director of the Office of Investing in Innovation at the United States Department of Education, wrote about the emerging patterns of impact in the hundreds of "i3" grants funded since 2010 (Mulhern, 2016). He has found interesting patterns in the evaluation and believes the nature of the partnerships may be a key factor. He sees success when practitioners and researchers work together. He does not see success when researchers *do* something to schools.

Our solution was to create a shared "big cycle" with the project director and coaches (university researchers) and the lead educators working with EL students in each district (practitioners). The agreed-upon core goal of this AI team is overall project implementation. Facilitation roles are shared. Though big in impact, the team is quite small with only six members. The process now feels collaborative and organic. Learning and adaptation happen and spread naturally. Good ideas are in charge, not an individual, and everyone doing the work has an important role in implementation.

A NOTE TO EVALUATORS—AND FUNDERS

The earliest glimmers and discussions of AI did grow out of frustration with the application of traditional evaluation methods (logic models and FOI indices) of developing projects, specifically the i3 grants referred to as "development grants." ED routinely requires the use of FOI, even when it is clear that they are funding "innovative" programming that encompasses new approaches. Other governmental and foundation funding sources are moving in the same direction of using FOI. This approach is written into the new "Education Innovation and Research" grant programs authorized under the Every Student Succeeds Act (2016).

The RtI evaluation (Balu et al., 2015) results brought about important fundamental questions about *how* schools are implementing RtI to improve student outcomes, *what* schools are doing with teacher training and monitoring, *when* schools are adjusting interventions based on student data, and *why* schools adjust or change practices. What this study does show is an excellent example of how—even under the best circumstances, where FOI was high (i.e., 86 percent of schools fully implemented RtI)—teaching and learning are complex processes with often no clear linear linkages to student achievement.

These highlighted studies are part of many similarly funded evaluation projects, where the Coalition for Evidenced-based Policy (2013) found that of the ninety interventions rigorously evaluated by the Institute of Education

Sciences (IES) since 2002, 88 percent had weak or nonsignificant findings and only 12 percent had positive findings. At the same time, schools are required to implement "evidence-based" practices and programs in which there are not that many for schools to utilize.

So, what are schools to do? At one end, there is a push for schools to use evidence and data. At the other end, there are not many practices and programs that have evidence. This quandary is at the heart of our work on AI.

Many programs and interventions are found to be ineffective at improving student outcomes, or worse, like the RtI study, to do harm to student outcomes. While these studies are important in answering whether or not a program or intervention worked to improve student outcomes, they do not lend themselves to direct application to practice. In study after study, results from both implementation and impact studies have not necessary improved our education system. Hence, measuring FOI is not particularly helpful to educational improvement in practice. Rather, documenting and testing teacher adaptation is very helpful as it could identify best practices that are field-tested in real "business as usual" settings.

Across the field of educational research, there is a missing piece. We are more aware of the need to measure FOI. We are also now very good at conducting rigorous impact studies. These implementation and impact studies have not acted as a magnifying glass to understanding the inner workings of schools, teacher instruction, and student learning. We know what works, but we do not know why. We know if an intervention was implemented with fidelity, but we do not know if that matters at all to the learning process. The missing piece in education is measuring AI.

AI is a much better way of applying a rigorous implementation framework to programs where you want and need to learn about the activities and strategies that work. While FOI tells a one-dimensional story as part of an evaluation, AI will provide you with a rich and detailed history of multiple ideas and paths taken. AI provides the context for each decision you made, explaining each successful strategy as well as each failure. The results of an AI process are far more valuable and provide far more guidance to the people who follow you down that same path.

Data experts, through researchers and evaluators, are a fundamental component to this AI process. You bring an especially important set of skills to the table that helps to keep the AI process grounded in data, where you,

- in step 1, help to establish waypoints because you conduct literature reviews of past research findings and conduct analysis of current data;
- in step 2, facilitate AI team meetings that identify resources, constraints, and opportunities because you are trained in conducting needs assessments;

- in step 3, lead the AI team in conducting a pro and con assessment of activities and creating the DAP, where your training in creating logic models come in handy;
- in step 4, annotate and describe what was (and what was not) implemented, keeping a keen eye on adaptations, because of your training and experience in multimethod data analysis; and
- in step 5, facilitate a discussion on lessons learned, what worked, and what might be done next time, where you bring a bias-free perspective to the discussion.

Field-based partnerships, where the goal is to help educators use data and research to improve a complex system, is hard work; it can often take time, and it challenges us to think differently about data (Bryk, 2009; Cohen-Vogel et al., 2015). There is still a place to conduct FOI studies, and a place to conduct random assignment studies. But when the focus is on developing and improving on a set of activities, similar to a development grant, an AI approach would better help facilitate a strong, ongoing researcher–practitioner partnership.

MAKING THE TIME

Back to our old-school wisdom: *What the head doesn't do, the feet do twice.* AI doesn't take time. It makes time as we increase our efficiency and stop endless repetitions of things that are not moving us closer to our goals.

Finding time for adults to meet and work together is a never-ending struggle in schools. Teachers and administrators are in a state of constant reaction to events, with little control or direction over their own days. There is a steady flow of "emergency" meetings and responses. Planning and reflection are viewed as luxuries and often get lost in the hectic and unpredictable course of time. Even when funding is provided for after-school meetings, participants are tired and stressed—hardly a conducive time for engaging and reflective planning work.

Do you see an opportunity to apply AI here? Of course you do! We have a known core goal: time for adults to work together. Our unknown is how to make that happen. The choices here are to find a way to learn and adapt, or to simply abandon the idea of making planning time happen.

AI teams generally meet every four to six weeks. A good rule of thumb is to allow enough time to do something and see something between meetings. For example, if you are trying a new instructional approach in your classroom, you want time to get comfortable with it *and* time to assess its impact on your students. If you are implementing a new school-wide student behavior program, you want to pause and reflect, identifying the need for adaptation before small problems become big problems.

There are dozens of excellent models in use by school districts throughout the nation that have quality time for planning built in, and that time is protected by the people who use it because it is important and useful to them. Reviewing those options is beyond the scope of this work, but it should be crystal clear that AI will not be successful unless there is an honest commitment to making the time for the team members to work together.

THE FINAL WORD: MOMENTUM

So what happened to Project ExcEL? Through the case study examples at each step, we hope we gave you a glimpse at our learning and improving process that can be challenging and dynamic, yet incredibly rewarding. We have had administrative changes, state policy changes, and even a record-setting snow that made getting to school difficult! Through all of these "business as usual" situations common in districts, we've been through multiple AI interactions, with a lot of learning and adapting along the way. Is it worth it? Absolutely. In one of the high schools, nineteen out of the twenty-one EL students passed the New York Regents Algebra I exam. This allowed the school to offer a dual-language trigonometry class for the first time in their history.

AI can be a little addicting, and once you embrace the process you do begin to see potential applications all around you. That is because AI is not just a process, it is a way of thinking about everything you do.

We've used the example of making dinner. Any parent knows this is an adaptive process, from dinosaur-shaped chicken nuggets to one day after reading *Charlotte's Web*, when your child proclaims to be a vegetarian. Parents cook, assess, adapt, and cook again. The core goal remains the same: to make healthy meals for the family. The waypoint is clear and defined: make some type of meal that has some protein, carbohydrates, and fiber. They look through recipes and cookbooks to figure out what they are going to make. They look at what they have, could have (if they go to the grocery store), and constraints (like food allergies).

Once dinner is complete and (happily?) eaten, the parent assesses how the meal was by looking at the child's plate or the smile on her face (and not by asking a series of survey questions on the quality of the meal). Culinary disaster? You might decide to try a different ingredient. Culinary success? You might set your sights on the next waypoint and start all over. But of course, you learned a lot along the way and have a collection of tried-and-true recipes for your family.

Teaching and learning are similar. We don't stop learning after our official training—our teacher preparation program—ends. We learn, share, and adapt each moment we interact with our students, parents, fellow educators, and administrators.

Changing the way you think is a process that takes work and practice. Having a structure that helps you engage in that activity, like a regularly scheduled AI team meeting, is the path to making that change. When you set goals that are important to you, you train and learn every day on your way to mastery.

Appendix

Adaptive Implementation Tools

Templates for the Adaptive Implementation Process

ADAPTIVE IMPLEMENTATION PROCESS TEMPLATE

Directions: This is the overview of the Adaptive Implementation (AI) cycle, the AI cycle graphic. The core goal is written in the center circle (black circle). A brief description of each step follows:

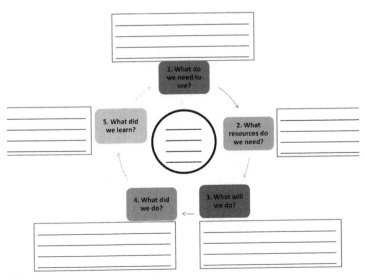

Figure A.1

ADAPTIVE IMPLEMENTATION SUMMARY GUIDE

Directions: This is a summary of the AI steps and tools. This is a helpful guide as you introduce the concept and process with the cycle graphic.

AI Steps	Description	Tools & Protocols
Core Goal	A core goal is a high-priority set by districts and schools for practitioners to implement.	
Step 1: What do we want to see?	Observable and measurable waypoints (outcomes) aligned with the core goal.	☐ Waypoint Checklist ☐ Waypoint Assessment Tool
Step 2: What resources do we have?	Resources include money, people, materials, and technology.	☐ AI Resource Management Tool
Step 3: What will we do?	A roadmap of activities that leads to the waypoint.	☐ Pro Con Assessment (PCA) ☐ Design and Action Plan (DAP)
Step 4: What did we do?	An annotation of the roadmap of activities to describe what and how it was done.	☐ Data Review Sheet
Step 5: What did we learn?	An honest assessment of what was done, what worked, what did not work, and what to do next.	☐ Discussion Protocol Tool

Figure A.2

STEP 1: WHAT DO WE WANT TO SEE? FIVE CHARACTERISTICS OF STRONG WAYPOINTS CHECKLIST

Directions: Use this checklist as a guide during the AI team discussions on waypoints.

Five Characteristics of Strong Waypoints

❑ They focus on things that are important to you.
❑ They focus on things you can do.
❑ They demand effort and new learning.
❑ They are built on evidence of student need.
❑ They are built by the people doing the work.

Figure A.3

STEP 1: WHAT DO WE WANT TO SEE?
WAYPOINT ASSESSMENT TOOL

Directions: During the AI team meeting to discuss and finalize the waypoint(s), use this assessment tool to ensure that everyone agrees and are excited about the waypoint. Write the waypoint at the top. Have each member of the AI team honestly assess what they think about it. Print this out on a larger sheet of paper. Each person on the AI team has a sticker (dot). They will put a dot in the corresponding location along the X-axis (the arrow). You are ready to move forward with the waypoint when everyone on the AI team hits close to the right-hand side.

Figure A.4

STEP 2: WHAT RESOURCES DO WE HAVE? ADAPTIVE IMPLEMENTATION RESOURCE MANAGEMENT TOOL

Directions: During the AI team meeting, use this resource tool to identify what you have, what you do not have, and what you could have within the following domains: (1) money, (2) people, (3) materials, and (4) technology.

Money

Carefully consider the type of money you're seeking to access or use. Examples include:

- Are you using grant money that can only be used for certain things?
- Are you following federal, state, and local audit guidelines in your proposed use of the money?
- Are there other funding sources that might cover the same things?
- Have you considered fundraising to create additional resources?

While money truly is just another tool to be used effectively and efficiently, it is a resource that requires conversations with fiscal/financial staff to ensure appropriate usage and effective tracking of expenditures.

What you have (Resources)	What you don't have (Constraints)	What you could have (Opportunities)

People

Carefully consider staffing needs over time.

- Unlike money, materials, or technology, staffing requires an extra measure of careful thought because it involves the well-being and security of people and their families.
- Whether you work in a union, right-to-work or other environment, you're entrusting people with important tasks that need to be matched with skills, commensurate pay and benefits, and a funding stream.
- While it may the norm in education to slide individuals around as grant funds and special pots of money become accessible, thereby bridging staffing and funding, it is not an effective way to recruit and retain committed professionals.

Does the intended role of a new staff member require highly specialized skills, or would this present an opportunity for community engagement and volunteer opportunities? Is there a community partner who could provide similar expertise?

What you have (Resources)	What you don't have (Constraints)	What you could have (Opportunities)

Figure A.5

Materials

Materials are often combined or conflated with money, but the need to split these two categories of resources is tantamount to understanding the nature of resources available to you.

- Materials may be included in the fees or funds expended when purchasing or obtaining models or packages of resources—don't be afraid to ask leaders and vendors what is included (is it digital? can you copy it?), when materials will be available, and what the cost of additional materials is. Get this in writing when feasible and appropriate.
- Materials may be available as donated goods or at a reduced price through local affiliates.
- Materials may have already been purchased or may be purchasable through extant purchasing agreements or existing programs. Don't duplicate efforts because you're afraid to ask.

Is there a community partner, state/federal office, or philanthropic organization tasked with providing resources in this area?

What you have (Resources)	What you don't have (Constraints)	What you could have (Opportunities)

Technology

While technology has traditionally been fetishized in educational circles and settings, it may help to plan for technology needs as if it is merely another type of material. However, given purchasing constraints and existing agreements, technology may need to be tracked separately based on your local context. Though used to frame technology here, the following questions can be used for the categories above as well:

- What critical need does the technology fill? Can this need be filled with extant resources?
- Is the technology worth it? It doesn't take many gimmicky do-dads to get to a full-time teacher's salary (especially when one adds in service contracts, extended warranties, etc.). Ensure that the technology adds real value.
- Again, is there another source that could fund this technology?

If the technology didn't exist, how would you do what you want to do without it? Is the answer more cumbersome than the purchasing process, the expenditure of funding, the training needed to effectively use the technology, and the need to maintain the technology?

What you have (Resources)	What you don't have (Constraints)	What you could have (Opportunities)

Figure A.5 *(cont.)*

STEP 3: WHAT WILL WE DO? PRO AND CON ASSESSMENT TEMPLATE

Directions: Write down the waypoint from step 1. Brainstorm activities that would lead you to this waypoint and list them in the Activities and Key Components column. Write down the pros and cons for each activity.

Waypoint: _____

_____

_____

_____

Activities and Key Components	Pros (Resources: Money, people, materials, technology)	Cons (Resources: Money, people, materials, technology)
Potential Activity: Describe _____ _____ _____ _____		
Potential Activity: Describe _____ _____ _____ _____		
Potential Activity: Describe		

Figure A.6

Potential Activity: Describe

Figure A.6 *(cont.)*

STEP 3: WHAT WILL WE DO? DESIGN AND ACTION PLAN TEMPLATE

Directions: Use this template as a framework to set up your self-adhesive notes. The resources are from step 2 on the left side. The waypoints are from step 3 on the right side. The key components and activities are from the pro and con assessment.

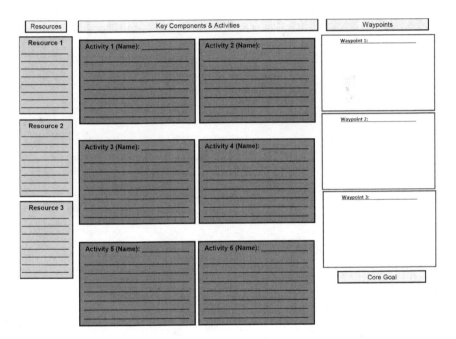

Figure A.7

STEP 4: WHAT DID WE DO? DATA REVIEW SHEET

Directions: During the AI team meeting, use this data review sheet as a way to analyze and synthesize the information collected from the AI team members. Write down the waypoint from step 1. Write down the key components and activities from the Design and Action Plan (DAP). As a team, assess whether the activities were done all the time, some of the time, or not at all. The notes section should describe important details that would help in the planning and learning process.

Waypoint: _____

Activities and Key Components	Yes: All the time	No: Some of the time	No: Not at all	Notes
Activity: Describe _____				
Activity: Describe _____				
Activity: Describe _____				

Figure A.8

Activity: Describe _____

Figure A.8 *(cont.)*

STEP 5: WHAT DID WE LEARN?
DISCUSSION PROTOCOL TOOL

Directions: During the AI team meeting, use this discussion protocol tool to show the three steps to the debrief meeting: (1) step 1: review, (2) step 2: assess, and (3) step 3: plan. Under each step, we have questions for the team to discuss.

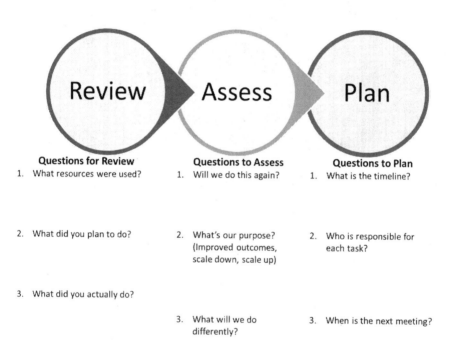

Questions for Review
1. What resources were used?

Questions to Assess
1. Will we do this again?

Questions to Plan
1. What is the timeline?

2. What did you plan to do?

2. What's our purpose? (Improved outcomes, scale down, scale up)

2. Who is responsible for each task?

3. What did you actually do?

3. What will we do differently?

3. When is the next meeting?

4. What worked?

5. How do you know it worked?

Figure A.9

References

Allensworth, E. M., & Easton, J. Q. (2007). *What Matters for Staying On-Track and Graduating in Chicago Public Schools: A Close Look at Course Grades, Failures, and Attendance in the Freshman Year.* Chicago, IL: CCSR. Retrieved from http://ccsr.uchicago.edu/publications/07%20What%20Matters%20Final.pdf

Balfanz, R., Herzog, L., & Mac Iver, D. J. (2007). Preventing student disengagement and keeping students on the graduation path in urban middle-grades schools: Early identification and effective interventions. *Educational Psychologist, 42*(4), 223–235.

Ball, D. L., & Cohen, D. K. (1996). Reform by the book: What is—or might be—the role of curriculum materials in teacher learning and instructional reform? *Educational Researcher, 25*(9), 6–14.

Balu, R., Zhu, P., Doolittle, F., Schiller, E., Jenkins, J., & Gersten, R. (2015). *Evaluation of Response to Intervention Practices for Elementary School Reading (NCEE 2016–4000).* Washington, DC: US Department of Education, Institute of Education Sciences, National Center for Education Evaluation and Regional Assistance.

Berman, P. (1978). *Designing Implementation to Match Policy Situation: A Contingency Analysis of Programmed and Adaptive Implementation.* Santa Monica, CA: RAND Corporation.

Bransford, J. D., Brown, A. L., & Cocking, R. R. (Eds.) (1999). *How People Learn: Brain, Mind, Experience, and School.* Washington, DC: National Academy Press.

Bryk, A. S. (2009). Support a science of performance improvement. *Phi Delta Kappan, 90*(8), 597–600.

Bryk, A. S. (2016). *Fidelity of Implementation: Is It the Right Concept?* Retrieved from https://www.carnegiefoundation.org/blog/fidelity-of-implementation-is-it-the-right-concept/

Bryk, A. S., Gomez, L. M., & Grunow, A. (2010). *Getting Ideas into Action: Building Networked Improvement Communities in Education.* Stanford, CA: Carnegie

Foundation. Retrieved from http://www.carnegiefoundation.org/spotlight/webinar-bryk-gomez-building-networked-improvement-communities-in-education

Bryk, A. S., Gomez, L. M., Grunow, A., & LeMahieu, P. G. (2015). *Learning to Improve: How America's Schools Can Get Better at Getting Better.* Cambridge, MA: Harvard Education Press.

Burns, M. K., Appleton, J. J., & Stehouwer, J. D. (2005). Meta-analytic review of responsiveness-to-intervention: Examining field-based and research-implemented models. *Journal of Psychoeducational Assessment, 23*(4), 381–394.

Cannata, M., & Nguyen, T. (2015). *Consensus versus clarity: Tensions in designing for scale.* Paper presented at the American Education Research Association, Chicago, IL.

Chingos, M. M., Whitehurst, G. J., & Lindquist, K. M. (2014). *School Superintendents: Vital or Irrelevant?* Washington, DC: Brookings Institute, Brown Center on Education Policy.

Coalition for Evidence-Based Policy. (2013). *Randomized Controlled Trials Commissioned by the Institute of Education Sciences Since 2002: How Many Found Positive Versus Weak or No Effects.* Washington, DC: Author.

Cohen-Vogel, L., Tichnor-Wagner, A., Allen, D., Harrison, C., Kainz, K., Socol, A. R., & Wang, Q. (2015). Implementing educational innovations at scale: Transforming researchers into continuous improvement scientists. *Educational Policy, 29*(1), 257–277.

Cohen, D. K., Raudenbush, S. W., & Ball, D. L. (2003). Resources, instruction, and research. *Education Evaluation and Policy Analysis, 25*(2), 119–142.

Collins, J. C., & Porras, J. I. (1994). *Built to Last: Successful Habits of Visionary Companies.* New York: HarperCollins Books.

Doran, G. T. (1981). There's a S.M.A.R.T. way to write management's goals and objectives. *Management Review, 70*(11), 35–36.

Dragoset, L., Thomas, J., Herrmann, M., Deke, J., James-Burdumy, S., Graczewski, C., Boyle, A., Upton, R., Tanenbaum, C., & Giffin, J. (2017). *School Improvement Grants: Implementation and Effectiveness (NCEE 2017–4013).* Washington, DC: National Center for Education Evaluation and Regional Assistance, Institute of Education Sciences, US Department of Education. Retrieved from https://ies.ed.gov/ncee/pubs/20174013/pdf/20174013.pdf

Duffy, F. M. (2003). Dancing on ice: Navigating change to create whole-district school improvement. *Organization Development Journal, 21*(1), 36–44.

Dusenbury, L., Brannigan, B., Falco, M., & Hansen, W. B. (2003). A review of research on fidelity of implementation: Implications for drug abuse prevention in school settings. *Health Education Research, 18*(2), 237–256.

Dweck, C. S. (2006). *Mindset: The New Psychology of Success.* New York: Random House.

Dwyer, M. C., Borman, J., Cervone, L., Fafard, M.-B., Frankel, S., Harvell, C., & Zarlengo, P. (2005). *Leadership Capacities for a Changing Environment: State and District Responses to the No Child Left Behind Act of 2001.* Providence, RI: The Education Alliance at Brown University.

Fixen, D. L., Naoom, S. F., Blase, K. A., Friedman, R. M., & Wallace, F. (2005). *Implementation Research: A Synthesis of the Literature (FMHI Publication #231)*. Tampa, FL: University of South Florida, Louis de la Parte Florida Mental Health Institute, The National Implementation Research Network.

Goodwin, B. (2015). *The Road Less Traveled: Changing Schools from the Inside Out*. Denver, CO: McREL International.

Grissom, J. A., & Andersen, S. (2012). Why superintendents turn over. *American Educational Research Journal, 49*(6), 1146–1180.

Heifetz, R. A., Grashow, A., & Linsky, M. (2009). *The Practice of Adaptive Leadership: Tools and Tactics for Changing Your Organization and the World*. Boston, MA: Harvard Business Press.

Hulleman, C. S., & Cordray, D. S. (2010). Moving from the lab to the field: The role of fidelity and achieved relative intervention strength. *Journal of Research on Educational Effectiveness, 2*(1), 88–110.

IDEO. (2012). *Design Thinking for Educators*. Riverdale, CA: Author.

Kekahio, W., Cicchinelli, L., Lawton, B., & Brandon, P. R. (2014). *Logic Models: A Tool for Effective Program Planning, Collaboration, and Monitoring (REL 2014–025)*. Washington, DC: US Department of Education, Institute of Education Sciences, National Center for Education Evaluation and Regional Assistance, Regional Educational Laboratory Pacific.

Kilbourne, A. M., Almirall, D., Eisenberg, D., Waxmonsky, J., Goodrich, D. E., Fortney, J. C., & Thomas, M. R. (2014). Protocol: Adaptive implementation of effective program trials (ADEPT): Cluster randomized SMART trial comparing a standard versus enhanced implementation strategy to improve outcomes of a mood disorders program. *Implementation Science, 9*(1), 1–32.

Lawton, B., Brandon, P. R., Cicchinelli, L., & Kekahio, W. (2014). *Logic Models: A Tool for Designing and Monitoring Program Evaluations (REL 2014–007)*. Washington, DC: US Department of Education, Institute of Education Sciences, National Center for Education Evaluation and Regional Assistance, Regional Educational Laboratory Pacific.

Lester, P. (2017). *Investing in Innovation (i3): Strong Start on Evaluating and Scaling Effective Programs, But Greater Flexibility Needed on Innovation*. Washington, DC: Social Innovation Research Center.

Madhavan, G. (2015). *Applied Minds: How Engineers Think*. New York: W.W. Norton.

Maehr, M. L., & Midgley, C. (1996). *Transforming School Cultures*. Boulder, CO: Westview Press.

Mulhern, S. S. (March 2016). *$1.6 Billion Investing in Innovation Proves Martin Buber Right*. Retrieved from https://medium.com/@shanemulhern/1-6-billion-investment-in-innovation-proves-martin-buber-right-3ca970318cc2#.57sp5m2mz

Neild, R. C. (2009). Falling off track during the transition to high school: What we know and what can be done. *The Future of Children, 19*(1), 53–76.

Otterness, J. (2009). Teaching and learning—It's not rocket science! *Phi Delta Kappan, 91*(2), 86–88.

Park, S., & Takahashi, S. (2013). *90-Day Cycle Handbook.* Stanford, CA: Carnegie Foundation for the Advancement of Teaching.

Park, S., Takahashi, S., & White, T. (2014). *Learning Teaching (LT) Program: Developing an Effective Teacher Feedback System, 90-Day Cycle Report.* Stanford, CA: Carnegie Foundation for the Advancement of Teaching.

Penuel, W. R., Allen, A. R., Farrell, C., & Coburn, C. (2015). Conceptualizing research-practice partnerships as joint work at boundaries. *Journal of Education of Students Placed at Risk, 20*(1–2), 182–197.

Seftor, N. (2016). *What Does It Mean When a Study Finds No Effects? (REL 2017–265).* Washington, DC: US Department of Education, Institute of Education Sciences, National Center for Education Evaluation and Regional Assistance. Retrieved from http://ies.ed.gov/ncee/edlabs

Thacker, T., Bell, J. S., & Schargel, F. P. (2009). School culture assessment. In T. Thacker, J. S. Bell, & F. P. Schargel (Eds.), *Creating School Cultures That Embrace Learning: What Successful Leaders Do* (pp. 45–56). Larchmont, NY: Eye on Education.

US Department of Education. (2017). *Investing in Innovation Fund (i3).* Washington, DC: US Department of Education, Office of Innovation and Improvement (OII).

Vernez, G., Karam, R., Mariano, L. T., & DeMartini, C. (2006). *Evaluating Comprehensive School Reform Models at Scale: Focus on Implementation.* Santa Monica, CA: RAND Corporation.

W.K. Kellogg Foundation. (1998). *Evaluation Handbook.* Battle Creek, MI: Author.

W.K. Kellogg Foundation. (2004). *Using Logic Models to Bring Together Planning, Evaluation, and Action: Logic Model Development Guide.* Battle Creek, MI: Author.

Werner, A. (2004). *Guide to Implementation Research.* Washington, DC: Urban Institute Press.

About the Authors

Ryoko Yamaguchi, PhD, is a researcher and former special education teacher with more than twenty-five years of experience in K–12 public education, focused on school improvement and effective practices to improve outcomes for underserved students.

Laureen Avery is a researcher, program manager, and former practitioner with more than thirty years of experience in K–12 public education, focused on policies and programs that improve outcomes for underserved students.

Jason Cervone, PhD, has more than a decade of experience focusing on building equity through policy and practice.

Lisa DiMartino has more than fifteen years of experience working with educators, administrators, and community organizations to improve student achievement through professional development and program evaluation.

Adam Hall is an education research and policy consultant. He has served the education community as an evaluator, technical assistance provider, and professional developer for over twenty years.